THE FIVE-MINUTE MOM'S CLUB

THE FIVE-MINUTE
MOM'S CLUB

105 TIPS TO MAKE
A MOM'S LIFE EASIER

Stephanie Vozza

FRANKLIN GREEN
PUBLISHING

With love to David, Christopher, and Nicholas
and to the sisterhood of busy moms

THE FIVE-MINUTE MOM'S CLUB
FRANKLIN GREEN PUBLISHING
500 Wilson Pike Circle, Suite 100
Brentwood, Tennessee 37027
www.franklingreenpublishing.com

Library of Congress Cataloging-in-Publication Data
Vozza, Stephanie, 1964-
 The five-minute mom's club : 105 tips to make a mom's life easier /
Stephanie Vozza.
     p. cm.
 ISBN 978-0-9826387-1-2 (pbk. : alk. paper)
 1. Mothers--Life skills guides. 2. Time management. 3. Parenting.
 4. Organization. I. Title.
 HQ759.V69 2010
 640'.43--dc22

                                                                    2010028997

 Printed in the United States of America
 1 2 3 4 5 6 7 8 9 10—15 14 13 12 11 10

CONTENTS

AUTHOR'S NOTE

While I love having five minutes to myself, my *favorite* five minutes of the day come when I tuck my boys into bed and tell them goodnight. The hustle and bustle of the day is behind us, and I can connect with each of my sons individually. I cherish this time. That's why I'm donating a percentage of the profits from this book to the Pajama Program (www.pajamaprogram.org). This wonderful not-for-profit organization gives warm pajamas and a new book to children in need, many awaiting adoption. I believe all children deserve a cozy bed and a bedtime story, and I hope you'll kiss your child goodnight tonight and think of the children this book will help.

Fondly,
Stephanie

ACKNOWLEDGMENTS

This book was a labor of love, but it wouldn't have happened without the help of many people. I would like to thank my publisher, Lee Gessner with Franklin Green Publishing, who calmed my (many) freakouts and believed in this project. Thanks to my editor Mary Sanford, who kept me on time and on task and who did a beautiful job laying out the pages. Thanks to Julie Ticknor, my cover designer. You did an amazing job creating our bird design all while raising two little birds! Thanks to my publicist Melissa Cassera, of Cassera Communications, who had amazing ideas and completely understood my mission.

I would like to thank the moms and experts who were generous with their advice: Laura Vanderkam, Aby Garvey, Gail Gray, Ellen R. Delap, Stacey Kannenberg, Debra Spears-Turner, Carley Knobloch, Kate Hare, Molly Gold, Alejandra Costello, Julie Morgenstern, Lorie Marrero, Nina Restieri, Angela Jia Kim, Kim Meinen, Dana Wood, Dimitri James, Susanna Romano, Aimee LaLiberte, Michelle LaRowe, Faun Zarge, Colleen McGee, Alicia Rockmore, Barbilee Hemmings, Kay Tomaszewski, Nancy Beck, Gretchen Rubin, Leigh Caldwell, Debbie Jordan, Kelly Novotny, Ashley Leeds, Alexandra Mayzler, Steve Boorstein, Jennifer Tankersley,

Erin Chase, Tracy Alt, Gigi Lewis, Elizabeth Goodsell, Aviva Goldfarb, Lindsay Ballard, and Candi Wingate.

Personally, I would like to thank my parents, Bill and Georgia, who supported this idea in more ways than one, and my sister Christina, who has always been my biggest cheerleader. I love you guys! A special acknowledgement to my Nana, who was the first writer in our family. I wish you were here to see this, but I know you are proud. Thanks to my Savor sisters, Angela (who came up with the friendly title), Jenn, Julie, Lora (my no-excuses accountability partner), Melissa, Payson, and Rachel. You ladies rock and are the most amazing support system a girl can have. And thanks to Costco and Trader Joe's, for feeding my family with your great frozen foods while I finished my book.

Most of all, I would like to thank my husband, David, for believing in me and for listening to me talk about this project . . . for months. I love you very much and am grateful for your support. And a special thank you to the boys who made me a mom, Christopher and Nicholas. I love you more than you'll ever know. Thanks for sharing me with my laptop for too many minutes this past year.

THE FIVE-MINUTE MOM'S CLUB

INTRODUCTION

Once upon a time (which means before I had children), I was organized. So organized! In my job at a daily newspaper, I was known as the reporter who never missed a deadline. My house was neat and tidy. My drawers and closets were pristine. And my calendar was full of activities, for which I was never late. I channeled my inner Martha almost every day—once, I even made my own crackers.

Clearly, I had too much time on my hands.

Then I had children, and life as I had once known it was gone forever. I was chronically late. I couldn't find my keys. And dinner? You want dinner *again*? You just had dinner last night!

Then came the day that will forever (at least in our family) be known as "*Where's My PB&J?* Day"

One sunny morning around 8 a.m., I dropped my oldest off at school and returned home . . . only to get a call from the school reminding me that he was going on a field trip. Right, I said. I knew I had signed the permission slip, and I also knew he was wearing his class T-shirt. What could this call possibly be about?

Well, it turns out that I had forgotten to pack a sack lunch for him, and the class wouldn't be back to school in time to eat in the cafeteria. *Oops.* It was Wednesday, which was "fried chicken day" in the cafeteria: the only day of the week my son bought lunch.

As I tried to explain the fried chicken confusion to the school secretary, she interrupted me to say that the bus was leaving. In ten minutes. So I grabbed my youngest, a loaf of bread, a jar of peanut butter, a bag of carrots, and some pretzels and made my way to school trying to beat the bus. Which I did. By. The. Skin. Of. My. Teeth.

Sitting in my car watching the bus pull away and cleaning up from the impromptu lunch prep, I wondered: Why could I easily juggle deadlines and stories and sources before I had children, but now that life was "simpler," I couldn't remember to pack a simple brown bag lunch?

I was certain that if I could just *get organized,* I would have the key to a happy home, so I searched for and found products that would help me organize the tasks that caused me the most stress: time management, meal planning, and delegating. I was so excited about these products that I created a store called The Organized Parent, where moms could find products to organize their lives.

Bliss, right? Not so fast.

It's five years later and guess what? Time management, meal planning, and delegating are *still* the tasks that cause me stress. I discovered that the silver bullet wasn't a tool or system that *changed me,* making me more organized around the task. Instead, the fix was a quick solution that changed the task, making it manageable so that I could spend my time on the things that really matter to me.

And that's the reason I wrote this book. Because I found some great solutions to problems that I think you might be having in your own home. And I got some great advice from real moms and experts that I'm so excited to share.

Are you ready to make life easier?

As my youngest son would say, "Let's do this thing!!"

Five-Minute Mom's Club Oath

As a member of the Five-Minute Mom's Club:

- *I promise* to listen to the inner voice that tells me what's important and what's not;

- *I promise* to ask for help when I need it;

- *I promise* not to do anything for my children that they can do for themselves (unless the act of doing so genuinely brings me joy);

- *I promise* to not over-schedule myself; and

- *I promise* to take at least five minutes each day to do something that nurtures my spirit and my soul.

ONE
Getting Started: Tools and Attitudes

1.   Let Go of "Super Mom"

A mythical creature has been wreaking havoc in homes for the past couple of decades: She's called Super Mom, and she can burp a baby, whip up gourmet cupcakes for a preschool class, and help a seventh grader solve the Pythagorean Theorem before the paint dries on her manicured nails. But like her Clark Kent counterpart, she isn't real. And she shouldn't be.

The truth is that today's mom is overwhelmed and often stressed. Harried Mom Syndrome is as prevalent as the common cold, and nearly two thirds of us feel there isn't enough time in the day to get things done. We wish we were more organized, but getting organized is just one more thing to put on our already full to-do list.

Enough already!

Before you can take the first step toward making your life easier, understand that *organized* does not mean *perfect*. Feeling like super mom isn't about having it all and doing it all. Feeling super, Mom, is about identifying your priorities and not wasting time on the things that just don't matter.

2.   Embrace What Works

So where do we start?

The expression "If it ain't broke, don't fix it," definitely applies here. List three areas of your family life that work well. Maybe you are good at spending time with your children. Perhaps you are always trying new recipes. Or maybe your house is clutter-free. Celebrate what's working right here:

1. _____

2. _____

3. _____

For those areas of your household that work, I'm giving you permission to skip those tips in this book. Don't waste your time trying something new. And don't waste time reading about new techniques that might cause you to second guess your successful methods. Just keep doing what you're doing.

3. Identify What Isn't Working

Let's shift our thoughts to what's not working. The tasks that motivated you to pick up this book: those tasks that cause you stress. Tasks often cause stress because we're not doing them well—or we're not doing them at all.

Which task isn't working for you? Maybe it's meal planning. How about getting your kids and yourself out the door each morning? Or is it grocery shopping with young children?

Making matters worse, perhaps your best friend can do your most stressful task in her sleep. People always compliment her on that task. And this makes you feel inadequate, which adds *more* stress to your stress. Sound familiar?

Let's just get it all out on paper. What are the tasks that make you want to pull out your hair?

1. _____

2. _____

3. _____

It's natural to assume that if you were more organized about performing the task, you would eliminate the stress. But I'm here to challenge that line of thinking.

Whatever the task may be, I'm asking you to pay attention to the stress. Consider it a friendly red flag. A helpful warning. It's friendly and helpful because it's telling you something about the task:

1. You don't enjoy it.

2. You aren't naturally good at it.

3. It's not important to you.

4. Some or all of the above.

And that's OK. Own it! Embrace it! Celebrate it! Wear it on a T-shirt! Tell the world: "I hate laundry and I just don't care if my whites are super white!!!!" In the grand scheme of things, the majority of household tasks that cause us stress really don't matter.

Whenever you start to feel the stress creeping in, look at your list of What's Working (tip #2). You are doing something right. Celebrate that instead of beating yourself up!

4.   Change the Task, Don't Change Yourself

Trying to become more organized around the tasks you listed in What Isn't Working (tip #3) is like trying to force a square peg into a round hole. It doesn't work; it only frustrates.

Instead of changing yourself to match the task, change the task to match your lifestyle, so you can spend your time on what's important to you.

5.   Spend Your Time Like It's Money

Mark Twain said, "Buy land. They're not making it anymore." The same holds true for time; it's a precious commodity. Each day is made up of a finite 24 hours. How you spend or save yours will directly affect your happiness.

My son recently got his first job, and he created a list of things he wanted to save his money for:

1. New snowboard

2. New snowboard jacket

3. Car

Unlike some who might spend money immediately on impulse items, such as video games or candy, my son found that saving money was easy for him as long as he kept looking at his list and kept his eye on the prize.

I want you to do the same thing with your timesaving strategies. Adopting several timesaving ideas just to cram more stuff into your day won't be rewarding. In fact, it will most likely lead to burnout and meltdown.

Write down three things that are important to you that you want to save time for:

1. _____

2. _____

3. _____

Whenever you start to feel that you are wasting time on a task that doesn't feel like a prize, look at your list. Be aware when less desirable items start to crowd out those tasks that are really important to you. When I start to feel stress, I think about what I'm saving time for and make sure I have enough time that day to do what I really want.

Here's my list:

1. *Spending an hour each day just talking to my husband*

2. *Spending time each day individually connecting with my boys*

3. *Spending time on me, improving my fitness*

6.   Think of Your Time in Week Blocks

Laura Vanderkam is a mother of two as well as the author of *168 Hours: You Have More Time Than You Think*. Her book explores the paradigm shift of looking at time in week blocks. While most people think of their time in 24-hour blocks, Laura says looking at our lives in weeks—168-hour blocks—is a better way to get a true picture of your life.

We live our lives in hours, she says. You may have a picture of who you are—writer, mother, wife, for example—but does the way you spend your hours match this vision?

Looking at life in 168-hour blocks is a useful paradigm shift, because—unlike the occasionally crunched weekday—well-planned blocks of 168 hours are big enough to accommodate full-time work, intense involvement with your family, rejuvenating leisure time, adequate sleep, and everything else that actually matters, she writes.

To get more out of your hours, Laura suggests using a time log (you can download a copy from her website at www.my168hours.com) to track your activities for a week. Similar to keeping a food log, this exercise gives you a good, hard look at where you spend your time . . . and where you don't. In fact, Laura says that most people don't have any idea how they spend their time.

According to Laura, most of your hours are a choice. You have to eat and sleep, of course, but beyond that, a lot of things are more negotiable. If the 168 hours in your week were a blank slate, how would you fill them? When you look at time in week blocks, making everything fit seems more doable than if you try to make everything fit in a day.

7. Stay Busy

My mom always told me if you want something done, give it to a busy person. This speaks to Newton's Law of Motion: a body in motion tends to stay in motion and an object at rest tends to stay at rest.

Ever notice that the more things you have to do, the better you are at completing each one of them?

8.   Be Mindful of Parkinson's Law

British writer C. Northcote Parkinson penned this rule: "Work expands to fill the time allotted."

In other words, if you have an hour to do a five-minute job, it will take an hour to do it. Keep this in mind when you start a task. Schedule not only a start time/date, but also an end time/date.

9.   Have an Accountability Partner

According to the folks at WebMD.com, dieters who find weight loss buddies (someone to share your work and goals) increase their odds for success versus those who go it alone. The same holds true when it comes to any lifestyle change.

If you decide to tackle a project, such as cleaning your garage or clearing out your child's old clothing, find another mom with a similar goal and tell her what you're going to do and by what deadline. You'll accomplish more than if you put the item on your list and let it slide.

10.   Don't Get Time-Jacked

Have you ever felt like a victim of time? I'm guilty of this myself. I'll think, "Oh, I wish I had time to go to the gym." Or "If I didn't have to do (fill in the blank), I'd have time to do (fill in the blank)."

The truth is that we all have exactly the same amount of time. We choose how to spend it. That bears repeating. We choose how we spend it. Are you spending your time on purpose? Or are you acting like a victim, at the mercy of time? When you spend your time on things that don't really matter to you, you take away time you could be using on things that do.

Let's commit to not wasting time on things that don't matter. Instead of spending too much time on things that you don't enjoy or aren't naturally good at and that aren't really important, let's adopt a quick solution.

11.   Do It Little and Often

Your first goal is to carve out an extra five minutes. You may be saying, "Five minutes? What can I possibly accomplish in five minutes? My sink is full of last night's dinner dishes. My toddler is throwing a tantrum. My cat just threw up. And my laundry has its own ZIP code. I can't possibly get anything done in five minutes."

Well, you'd be surprised. Set your kitchen timer or the stopwatch on your phone for one minute. Now sit quietly until it beeps. Feels like a nice little chunk of time, huh? Or how about putting an unruly five-year-old into a five-minute time out, then tell me how long that felt. An eternity, right? Whether you break tasks down into bite-sized pieces or implement five-minute solutions, five minutes is actually plenty of time to get things done.

In his book, *Do It Tomorrow*, Mark Forster says the human mind works best when it does something "little and often." In other words, five-minute bites will help you tackle any big project more effectively than trying to do great bursts of action (which often leads to burnout).

Five Things You Can Do in Five Minutes

As moms, just think of all of the time we spend waiting: in the carpool line, at the orthodontist's office, during soccer practice, at dance lessons, on parent-teacher conference night. Here are five quick things to do in those minutes waiting.

1. Quick phone calls that can easily be forgotten: Make doctor and dentist appointments for the family. Call and book your next haircut. Get an appointment for car maintenance. Call the babysitter. Schedule your pet's vet visit. Get price quotes for a job you want to hire out, such as carpet cleaning or painting. Call about a discrepancy in a bill. Or call that chatty friend who is hard to hang up on—now you have a good reason for making it short and sweet.

2. Read the mail: Create a car bag with catalogs, magazines, and product/company brochures that you don't have time to read and bring it with you when you leave the house. Five minutes is enough time to flip through most catalogs. It's also enough time to read an article in your favorite monthly magazine.

3. Clear car clutter: Five minutes may be all you need to clean out your glove compartment or car console. Bring a trash bag with you and declutter your car. Gather things that don't belong in the car, and when you return home,

put them away. This is a good time to make a list of items you'd like to keep in your car, such as a cooler, for transporting frozen food home from the grocery store; jackets, for nights that get chillier than expected; a blanket, for keeping warm or for an impromptu picnic; a first-aid kit, for minor injuries on the road; or portable chairs, for sporting events.

4. Save money: With food prices climbing, clipping coupons has never made more sense. Most people who don't clip say that the time involved is their reason for passing on the savings. Bring the coupon flyers from your paper or mail and a pair of scissors. Take five minutes to clip away. Be sure to have a good coupon organizer. You can also use this time to go through your coupons and discard those that have expired.

5. Make your lists: Grocery lists. To-do lists. Errand lists. Chore lists. Smart moms are not listless! Plan your meals for the week and then create your grocery list. Bring your calendar with you and make a to-do list that gets you prepared for everything on this week's schedule. And create job lists for your children. It's easier to delegate work when it's written down.

12.   Do Some, It's Better Than None

Aby Garvey is a mom as well as the co-owner of Simplify101.com, a professional organizing business that specializes in online organizing workshops. She believes organizing can be creative and fun. "The more you love an organizing solution the more likely you are to use it," she says. Here's her advice for tackling big projects:

> When it comes to getting organized and clearing out clutter, remember that some progress is better than no progress. In short: some is better than none.
>
> The beginning of any big project can be hard. That end point can seem so far away that it's sometimes difficult to muster up the energy to even get started. You think, I couldn't possibly get it all done today, so you don't begin today . . . or tomorrow . . . or the day after that.
>
> This form of "all or nothing" thinking—I can't clean out the entire garage today so I'll wait to begin—can keep you indefinitely stuck in inaction. Keep this in mind: you can't finish something until you start it. So just focus on getting started; the finishing will fall into place.
>
> Whenever you find yourself avoiding the start of a big project—organizing or otherwise—remember the catchy little phrase "some is better than none." You don't have to finish the entire project today, but you could get started today. Progress you make today is a step in the right direction—a step closer to done!

13.   How to Find Time

Do you feel time-starved? There are pockets of time everywhere if you just look.

Here are five places to find a spare five minutes:

1. Beginning of the day
2. End of the day
3. While you're waiting
4. In the shower
5. During your child's nap (if your child doesn't nap, implement personal me time)

Here are five more:

1. While you are sleeping (trust me on this one . . . I'll get to it later)
2. While you are watching television
3. While you are sitting in traffic
4. While you are cooking dinner
5. While you are on the phone with a long-winded friend

Once you start rethinking your time, you'll find five-minute pockets everywhere. I'm sure you can think of dozens more. I encourage you to let some of these five-minute blocks tick away in peace. Others, you might take advantage of and fill with bite-sized chores.

14. Choose Actions Over Distractions

Some tasks and habits seem harmless enough. But they are actually distractions (a.k.a. time wasters). You know, the activity that will take just a second and ends up with you saying, "Oh, my. Where did the time go?"

Here are ten distractions:

1. Surfing the web
2. Watching television

3. Talking on the phone
4. Rambling
5. Procrastination
6. Doing something for someone else when they should be doing it themselves
7. Explaining your answer
8. Not taking the time to do it right the first time
9. Looking for misplaced items
10. Not having a plan

How much time have you wasted going back to the grocery store because you forgot one item for tomorrow's dinner? Or, honestly, how much time do you waste on the Internet? Or how about the time you waste giving a long-winded explanation of why you can't volunteer for another school committee when a simple "I'm sorry, but I'm just not available this time" will suffice.

One quick tip: When it comes to watching television, if you have a DVR, you can use it to save time. I know a family that likes to watch *American Idol* together. Instead of sitting down when it starts, they set their DVR to record it and work on other tasks. Then, when the show is about 20 minutes in, they sit down and watch, fast-forwarding through the commercials. They are generally able to see the end right on time and can talk about the show the next day with everyone else.

That said, here's one quick warning: Owning a DVR may actually increase the time you spend time watching television. A survey by Nielson reports that DVR owners watch 29 percent more TV than non-DVR owners.

15. Rethink Your To-Do List

A lot of moms tell me that their to-do list is as long as a child's list to Santa. The more items on your list, the better the chance you will feel overwhelmed and the better the chance that you'll get nothing done. Long lists can be counterproductive unless you look at yours in a different way.

Let's start by getting out that to-do list. If you have already created one, grab it. If you are too overwhelmed to even have a list, it's time to write one. The feeling of being overwhelmed often occurs when your perceived list is longer than your actual list. It's easier to look at tasks objectively if you write them down. Get them out of your head and onto paper. It's almost always not as bad as you imagine.

So go ahead and write down everything you *think* you have to do. Notice the word *think*. We're going to start moving things around. We're going to look at your tasks through "3-D glasses."

OK, now that you have your to-do list, we're going to get to work. Grab a new piece of paper, and at the top, write down these three words: *Don't, Delegate,* and *Do.* This is your new to-do list.

16. Don't

The *Don't* category on your to-do list is where you list the items you thought you had to do, but after closer examination, you discover that you really don't have to do. This is my favorite category!

Coco Chanel gave women this fashion advice: Before you leave the house, look in the mirror and remove one thing. We're going to apply Coco's advice with the Don't category of our list. (Don't you feel chic and powerful just thinking about it?!)

Look at your tasks and identify the ones that cause you stress. Now ask yourself, What would happen if I don't do it? Sometimes the stress is really guilt about something we think we *should* do. If the result of not doing the task is less stressful than the task itself, put it on your *Don't* list.

For example, maybe you make your child's bed when you make your own. It's easy to get into the habit of doing something for your child that they can do for

Don't Forget to Don't

Need help knowing when to say when? Here's a B.U.S.Y. Mom checklist:

Before U Say Yes, ask yourself:

- Am I saying yes because I would feel guilty if I said no?
- Is my gut reaction to this request "how can I get out of this?"
- Am I saying yes because I am known as the mom who always says yes?
- Am I saying yes because my friends have said yes?
- Will this event bring stress to my family life?
- When the event is done, will I be most glad that it's over?

If you answered yes to any of these questions, you should not say yes to this request of your time. Remember: It's OK to say NO.

themselves. I recently broke myself of my habit of making my boys' beds each morning. I reasoned that while I was making my own, it was simpler to just make theirs, too, so that my whole house was neat and tidy. This quick act took just a few minutes, but those few minutes meant that I had to remind my boys to make their beds on the weekend. I was taking that task out of their routine.

Maybe you are an overachieving volunteer at your child's school. If you truly enjoy it, that's fine. Schools would be lost without mom volunteers. But if you ever wish they would stop calling you (they won't, by the way) then you need to put excessive volunteering on your *Don't* list. At the very least, quantify the item so you know when you've had enough and when it's time to tell yourself, "Don't."

This follows the all-things-in-moderation way of thinking. Think of your favorite dessert. Me? I love cherry pie. But if I ate an entire pie, I would not be feeling the love. In fact, I might start to hate cherry pie. I might even resent the person who had left an entire cherry pie alone with a serious cherry pie fan. And then I would probably avoid cherry pie for a long time. Which would be sad. It's not the pie's fault. It's still delicious pie. But overindulging can change your perspective on things.

This same thinking applies to tasks. You might love to volunteer at your child's school, but if you're there as much as the staff, you might start to feel a little taken advantage of, underappreciated, and maybe even a little surly. It's not the school's fault—you overindulged. So set limits before this happens. Under the *Don't* category, write down something like this: "Don't sign up for more than one committee at a time," or "Don't volunteer to work the kindergarten art center during glitter season . . . ever again!"

Don't is also an important strategy when it comes to methods of completing tasks. For example, I have a friend who loves to cook a week's worth of meals on Sunday and freeze them. She is uber-organized when it comes to meal planning. Each night at 5 p.m. she takes something out of her freezer, pops it into the oven, and by 6 p.m. she's ready to serve dinner. Oh, how I wanted to feel that same joy. So I tried it. Instead of feeling relief, I felt stress. I really don't like cooking, so to consume an entire afternoon with bubbling pots and portioned dishes just made me feel bad. So I put freezer cooking on my *Don't* list.

There is not one way to do something. In fact there are as many methods to getting something done as there are people to do it. The goal is to complete the tasks you don't enjoy with a quick solution. And there are several quick solutions if you look.

Think about the tasks that cause you stress and think about the way you are completing those tasks. Is your method the cause of your madness?

17. Delegate

The *Delegate* category is where we move the things we were going to do to someone else's to-do list. This can be a new chore you assign your child, an errand you ask your husband to do on his way home, or ironing that you hire out.

This might just be the hardest category of your list to complete. That's because there is an art to delegating. Some moms have it and some don't. And the reason many moms aren't good at it is because we're hung up on having things done a certain way: Our way. *It's my way or the highway.* Sound familiar? I'm a control freak mom, so delegating doesn't come naturally to me. Especially when the completed job doesn't live up to my expectations. Often it feels easier if I just do it myself. But we all know that in the long run it isn't. Imagine if you visited your child's classroom and found the teacher sitting at a student's desk, finishing their homework. Sounds absurd, right? Of course! But when you do tasks for your child that they can do for themselves, it's the same thing.

Another reason delegating can be difficult for moms is because we are unaccustomed to or uncomfortable with the role of delegator. My dad worked in the automotive industry for more than thirty years. He told me that the best workers were often the worst managers. Why? Because their reaction to problems and glitches was often to jump in and do the job themselves. This created a vicious cycle of poor production, because the rest of the workforce wasn't being managed and motivated. Good worker = poor delegator.

This same idea can be applied to "managing" a household. If you delegate jobs to your family and they don't live up to your standards, do you jump in and finish or redo the job?

When you delegate tasks, remind yourself that it's not your job to *do* the tasks, your job is to *delegate* them. Stay focused on your job. I learned this lesson several years ago at a neighborhood party. A friend of mine was on the planning committee for our yearly subdivision party. She called me and asked if I would work the beverage table for an hour-long shift. I agreed. While I sat at the table that hot day, making sure kids didn't spill soda all over the place, I saw that my friend was having fun socializing under the shaded tent. I was surprised to learn that she didn't work any shifts at any of the party stations. *Humph!* I thought at the time. *If I had been on that committee, I would have signed up for one of the shifts before I gathered volunteers.* I realize now that her job wasn't to take a shift but to find others who would fill the shifts. Delegation: It can be the key factor between enjoying an event and feeling burdened by an event.

Take Time to Make Time

Gail Gray of Fresh Start Professional Organizing told me "It takes time to make time." *(Did you just have an a-ha moment? I did!)* I knew this was an obstacle for me, and I'm guessing it's an obstacle for other busy moms. Instead of taking the time to teach kids to do something, we quickly do it ourselves.

Gail was kind enough to share some advice for busy moms. Here are her thoughts on how it takes time to make time:

> Teaching others to do things for you is vital in making time! We tend to think it will be faster to just do it

ourselves, but if we take the time to train others to do it once, they can do it over and over again for us, saving us time in the long run. This includes our children. If we teach them how to do things around the home, including laundry, picking up after themselves, making lunches, getting things for themselves, it will save you time. Just think how each task we do for our kids (that they can do themselves) adds up to time away from doing other things. Taking the time to teach them to take care of themselves takes time, but it is worth the time saved in the long run.

Think of Delegating as "Team Building"

Ellen R. Delap is owner of Professional-Organizer.com, mom of two and grandmother of three. She says focusing on her family has always been a top priority. As a result, she calls delegating "team building," which makes it sound easier already! Here is her advice for making it work:

> You come home after work and there's always more to do than time to do it. Gather your family around you and think delegate, a.k.a. team building!
>
> There are a few ground rules at home that don't apply at the office. The complexity of family relationships makes delegating at home more challenging than at work. But it is not impossible. Truly applying team building makes this happen!
>
> Begin with the family motto of "we're all in this together!" Start with a family meeting to talk about what this means. Keep it simple but think through all the responsibilities at home and create a list of the options. There are lunches and dinner to make, groceries to buy, laundry to do, lawns to mow, toilets to

clean, and more. So getting a list together that hits on the most important tasks is a starting point. Here is where we start being creative!

Work from family members' strengths. Who is great at what? Give your family jobs they do well rather than struggle with.

Give the chores different point values by "difficulty" of completion. Bathroom and toilet 3 points, kitchen clean up 2, dusting 1.

Create partnerships to complete the chores, such as mom/sister make the dinner, dad/other daughter do the dishes. It is always more fun with a partner.

Set a time that everyone does the same task. Set the kitchen timer, turn on the high-energy music, or sing a clean up song. Set a standard of completion everyone agrees on. What does it mean to have the dishes "done" or the laundry "complete"? Set a time frame for completion. Emptying the dishwasher after the dishes are piled in the sink defeats the purpose.

Put aside your perfectionism. Encourage your family to do their best job, even if it is not to your standards, the manner in which you would do it, or at the speed you would do it.

Affirm each family member's contribution each week. Praise goes a long way in getting things done.

Create a chores chart and post it in a common space. It is the chart that reminds the family, rather than the parents.

Incentivize your family's work. Incentives can be whatever works for you, but the simpler the better.

Use this method for everyday responsibilities and upcoming family events, including holidays, birthdays, and special occasions.

Make it fun! Everyone wants to work together when the atmosphere is relaxed and happy.

Delegate by Hiring Tasks Out

Stacey Kannenberg is mom to two grade-school-aged daughters, CEO of Cedar Valley Publishing, and principal in Mom Central Consulting. Even more impressive is the fact that she's a master at delegation through outsourcing and network building. Here's her story:

> The ability to outsource is key for me! I can't do everything, so I have given up the things I absolutely don't like to do. I'm a clean freak who used to vacuum daily. Now I have cleaning help every Tuesday. Deanna does all the heavy cleaning and I do daily spot cleaning. A clean house makes me a happy and productive mom. Brenda cooks three dishes a week for us. They are lowfat and precooked from scratch, so we are always 1 minute and 30 seconds away from a meal. She does all the grocery shopping and prep work for those meals. She cooks for a few of my friends, so the price is much more reasonable because she buys and cooks in bulk. She delivers our meals on Tuesday mornings. She also comes for a few hours weekly and folds laundry, decorates for the new season, and organizes closets. It's the best $70 bill for the week. She saves me time that I can devote to my office and kids. And her meals save me time at the grocery store. I just need to get milk, fruit, cheese, bread, and other staples and out the door I go! Lynn does all my weeding and trimming to make my bushes and roses look great for roughly $150 for the summer.
>
> We also have a contingent of girls who watch our girls. Our neighbor Amanda is great for a quick

Speak Your Child's "Secret" Delegation Language

Do you wish your child would help around the house more often? Would you like to stop reminding your child what he or she needs to do?

It's much easier to delegate tasks to your child if you speak their language. Start by identifying your child's learning style, which is an approach to learning that works with someone's personality, preferences, and strengths. Look at these lists of traits. Check the statements that best describe your child:

The Visual Learner
☐ Loves puzzles and building with blocks or Legos
☐ Can be very sensitive to sound, light, and touch (often needs tags cut out of clothes)
☐ Can be very sensitive to criticism
☐ Is empathetic to the emotions of others
☐ Enjoys art and drawing
☐ Is good at reading maps, charts, and diagrams
☐ Likes mazes and puzzles
☐ Notices detail
☐ Has good eye-hand coordination
☐ Is often quiet and thoughtful
☐ Can have a vivid imagination
☐ Has trouble remembering verbal directions and messages

TOTAL VISUAL TRAITS ____

The Auditory Learner
☐ Is verbal at an early age
☐ Learns to do new things in steps, from easy to difficult
☐ Likes a predictable schedule
☐ Likes to tell stories and jokes
☐ Likes to play word games
☐ Loves to talk, even to him/herself

- [ ] Hums
- [ ] Asks lots of questions
- [ ] Is a good listener
- [ ] Makes noise if it's too quiet
- [ ] Can be distracted by too many sounds at one time
- [ ] Is very social

TOTAL AUDITORY TRAITS ____

The Tactile Learner
- [ ] Loves games and group activities
- [ ] Operates best with hands-on activities
- [ ] Needs things to be repeated
- [ ] Needs to handle something and try it out
- [ ] Has a short attention span
- [ ] Has a hard time sitting still
- [ ] Shows you things rather than telling you about them
- [ ] Seems to be in constant motion
- [ ] Is well coordinated
- [ ] Crawls and walks at an early age
- [ ] Likes to go first
- [ ] Takes things apart

TOTAL TACTILE TRAITS ____

Count the total number of checkmarks for each style and determine which has the highest number of matching traits. Remember, your child will possess a mixture of styles, but one style should be dominant.

Now tailor the tasks you assign your child to his or her strengths. Visual children will do well with tasks that involve detail. Assign the chores with written lists or text messages. Auditory children work best when they listen to music or have a partner with whom they can talk. Give an auditory child verbal directions. Tactile children like hands-on work. Give him or her verbal directions, but have them write things down themselves.

errand. Samantha is our college-bound summer help who has a car and can take the girls to the beach, basketball and/or volleyball camp, or swim lessons. I also have Katie, a teller at my bank, who can come before work for me during the school year. She can be at the house in the early morning, when my husband needs to leave for work and I am traveling, and take the girls to school.

It takes everyone in the family to be involved and a crew of people to pull it off—but it works for us! And I like the fact that I am helping other girls save for college and supporting moms who love to cook, clean, and garden.

18.   Create a To-Do List

Under the *Do* category, we're going to list what's left. Those things that you positively, absolutely, without a doubt must do yourself. Now that you've looked at this list, are you sure about each and every item? Positively? Absolutely? No doubt in your mind? OK, then. If you can accomplish only one thing today, what would that be? Circle it, and that's your list for today. Just one item on your to do list looks very doable, doesn't it? And just imagine the joy you would feel if you got that one thing done.

I know what you're saying: your to-do list is much longer than one item. And I understand. The idea is to think of your day in bite-sized pieces. A long list is overwhelming. One task at a time is manageable.

I have a whiteboard in my kitchen that I call my "one thing and one thing only" whiteboard. This is where I list the one thing I am going to accomplish today. And I love, love, love to erase it when I'm done!

If you've completed that one thing and you have time to tackle another, choose something else and circle it. Write it on your whiteboard. The important thing to remember is this: finish that first thing before you start a second, and so on.

Let me tell you about my dog, Dee Dee. Sometimes we call her "Speedy Dee Dee." Sometimes we call her "Greedy Dee Dee." And sometimes we call her "A Dee Dee." This is because she starts a lot of things but rarely finishes them before starting something else. For example, when she needs to go outside, she'll run full speed to the front yard, start to go to the bathroom, get distracted by a bird, chase the bird, and then decide she wants to come back inside . . . only to need to go outside twenty minutes later because she needs to go to the bathroom again. (Please note: I never dreamt that I would be discussing my dog's bathroom habits in print. And while I apologize, I have to admit that it definitely provides a colorful illustration.)

Some days I feel like Dee Dee. Easily distracted and accomplishing nothing. If you put one thing on your to-do list and do finish that one thing before you start another, I promise you will get more done than if you try to empty your bladder while chasing a bird.

Highlight Your Own Best Practices

Once you have that one item in your *Do* list, think about how you will complete it. We are going to talk about five-minute solutions to the most common stress-causing tasks, but sometimes the best answer for you will be a method you use to complete another task, something you already do well or enjoy doing.

Perhaps you're good at grocery shopping. You always have a list, broken down by where you find it in your store. You have checked your sale circular and matched specials with coupons. You are the Queen of the Aisle.

Think about how you do what you do. Is there a technique you are using that you could transfer to another task that you don't feel quite so confident about? If your grocery store strategy is to take a half hour on a Sunday afternoon with the grocery store circulars and your coupon organizer, chart out your savings, then go to the store and get your food for the week, then ask yourself, How can I apply this technique to laundry? Instead of doing a load a day and feeling like you're always doing laundry, why not take a Sunday night and knock it all out in one marathon session?

Instead of reinventing the wheel with every task, embrace your strengths and try to apply those skills to other tasks.

Create a To-Do-a-Go-Go List

Now, I want you to create your to-do-a-go-go list. "To-do-a-what-what?"

Here's what I mean: Go back to your original *Do* list and find the items that take just a minute or two. Maybe it's making an appointment to get a haircut. Maybe it's writing a thank you card. Or maybe it's clipping coupons from this week's newspaper. Anything that takes less than five minutes should go on your to-do-a-go-go list. Once you've got this list assembled, grab any supplies you might need (phone numbers, note cards, pens, stamps, scissors, coupon organizer, newspaper, etc.) and toss them in your car bag (more on this later) or in your purse. Now, when you're sitting in the carpool line, waiting at the orthodontist's office, or hanging out at hockey practice, take advantage of the time and accomplish one or more of these tiny to-go tasks. (*Note:* Please do not make phone calls while you drive. Only use your cell phone when you are in a parking lot!)

19.   Multitasking Is a Myth

So this leads us to the idea of multitasking, doing more than one thing at one time. You may think you're a master of multitasking. But research shows that the more you multitask, the worse you are at all of the tasks you're trying to accomplish.

In a 2009 study at Stanford University, researchers tested the theory with media multitaskers. You know, people who watch TV . . . while they tweet . . . while they read email. Turns out the more you multitask, the less you actually accomplish and retain.

The study reported: "People who are regularly bombarded with several streams of electronic information do not pay attention, control their memory or switch from one job to another as well as those who prefer to complete one task at a time."

A 2004 study at the University of Michigan found

that when people tried to multitask, it took longer to accomplish the tasks than if they did them separately. This is because the brain has to reorient to each new task, adding time to completion.

The study noted that for certain tasks that don't require thinking (eating while reading the paper, for example), the results weren't as significant. Although I have to add that when I combine eating with another task, I almost always eat more than I had planned. If you decide to work while you eat, you might want to consider portion control!

Multitask: Mom Style

Is multitasking ever a good idea? It can be. Especially when you are combining tasks with guilty pleasures, such as watching television. I try to make the most of my TV-watching minutes by folding laundry, clipping coupons, ironing, cleaning out my filing system, or dusting the family room.

Another way you can successfully multitask is when you need to physically be in a location but you don't need to give the activity your undivided attention. For example, while you wait for your child to finish their sports practice you can page through the magazines that are starting to pile up.

Debra Spears-Turner is a proud mom of two little girls as well as human resources manager and general counsel for a software company. She also does part-time work on the side as a staff attorney for a small law firm. Here's how she multitasks:

> I am definitely short on time, and as a result, I have learned to multitask and squeeze chores into times some people may not think of. I clean the bathroom while my girls bathe. I can quickly clean everything in about 15 minutes while staying right there with them. Once they are out of the tub and getting in their pajamas (with the help of my husband), I quickly clean the tub.

Of course you want to give your infant and toddler your undivided attention during bath time, but when children are older and need more supervision than actual hands-on care, this method works.

It's also multitasking when you throw a load of laundry in the washing machine and then vacuum while you wait until it's time to put the clothes in the dryer.

20.   Don't Multitask, Batch

I want you to meet Carley Knobloch. Life coach, productivity expert, and founder of Mothercraftcoaching.com, Carley admits that she's obsessed with helping moms feel less overwhelmed while getting more done. She and her husband, Mike, run a busy household with eight-year-old son Spencer, four-year-old daughter Annie, and Jenny, their Springer spaniel. One of her secrets is batching:

> Last night, as I wrote "Buy 8-year-old boy birthday present" on my errands list, I did some gruesome math. My kids each have about 20 classmates. If I spend about 45 minutes of my time buying them each a birthday present over the course of the school year (driving to the toy store about 10 minutes away, parking, browsing, waiting in line, and a 10-minute commute home) that's 30 hours of my life lost. Holy &#*$!

Instead of (literally) driving yourself insane, consider Batching Tasks: grouping together a bunch of similar to-dos and getting them done without interruption. Every time we switch tasks—from an email to a phone call, to the laundry, back to emails, then to cooking—we lose focus (and time and money, in the case of my birthday present debacle!), so it takes us longer to recover and get it done. Batching similar tasks together means tons more speed and efficiency. Sure, you could pay your electric bill in 3 minutes, but while you've got the checkbook, stamps, and envelopes out, you could probably pay a big pile of bills and write a a couple thank you cards in about the same amount of time.

Here are some ideas of tasks you could batch:

- Cook double portions for dinner and freeze one for another night's meal.

- Wash and prep ALL your vegetables when you get home from the grocery store, so they're ready to eat or cook.

- Give your Blackberry a rest and only check your email two times a day. (Yes, it's possible!)

- Put all your filing in a "To Be Filed" bin and get all the filing done while watching *So You Think You Can Dance.*

- Schedule all your medical appointments for one day.

- Address, stamp, and write all the birthday cards you want to send for the entire month in one night.

- Pack non-perishable snacks in reusable baggies once a week so part of lunch is already made.

- Buy 10 birthday presents instead of one and wrap them all at once so you're ready for multiple birthday parties.

The Tools

If you are ready to put these tips into action, here are some supplies you might consider:

1. Notepad for sorting your Don't, Delegate, and Do items.
2. Clipboard for taking your lists on the go.
3. Errand organizer, such as a small accordion file, for organizing your To-Do-a-Go-Go list supplies.
4. Whiteboard or chalkboard for posting your one "Must Do" for the day.
5. A timer, to avoid Parkinson's Law.
6. Delegating tools, such as a dry erase door hanger or stick-on whiteboard for assigning chores to visual children, recordable message center to assign chores to auditory children or clipboard to have tactile children record their chores and check them off as completed.

TWO
Time Management: Routines and Schedules

21.   Become a Well-Oiled Machine

The two most important tools for time-management success are a routine and a plan. According to Merriam-Webster, a routine is a "regular course of procedure; a habitual or mechanical performance of an established procedure."

You might think of a routine as a schedule, but according to a report by Vanderbilt University's Center on the Social and Emotional Foundations for Early Learning, the two have different meanings: "Schedules represent the big picture—the main activities to be completed daily. Routines represent the steps done to complete the schedule."

A "routine" sounds kind of boring, right? Perhaps, but a good routine is a mom's best friend. The Vanderbilt report states that routines are important because they influence a child's emotional, cognitive, and social development; they help children feel secure; they help children understand expectations; they help reduce behavior problems; and they can result in higher rates of child engagement. While the report was designed for college students studying early learning, these principles apply to a home setting as well.

The more routines you can put into place, the more your home will resemble a well-oiled machine. Here are some ideas of where to start: mornings, naps, meals, homework, chores, hygiene, and bedtime. Creating a routine is simple. Make a list of what needs to be done, delegate responsibilities (see tip #22), and implement.

Sticking to a time-management routine—much like sticking to an exercise routine—is where the difficulty lies. It might take a little time to get your routine in place, but once you do, your home can run on autopilot.

22.   Don't Be a "'TomTom' Mom"

While routines are the path to time-management success, delegating the responsibility for the tasks within the routine is key. This might be difficult for some moms. Like me. I have a confession to make: I have TomTom tendencies. I feel the need to stand over my children calling out directions like a GPS system.

I could never figure out why my boys wouldn't remember to brush their teeth if I didn't tell them. And then it dawned on me as I was maneuvering the streets of Chicago using a GPS to find my way on the second day of a conference. Although I had been to the same location the day before, I couldn't find the destination again because I wasn't learning the route; I was simply reacting to the commands.

Pulling the plug on GPS parenting isn't easy. Kids might feel lost at first, but it is possible to show them the way and put them on autopilot. Here's how:

Think of your own morning routine, for example. You most likely do the same things each morning, perhaps even in the same order, without even thinking about it (and hopefully without being told!). This is a routine, a habit. Establishing a routine takes time—about three weeks, actually.

Dr. Maxwell Maltz, author of *Psycho-Cybernetics,* discovered this technique: devote fifteen minutes a day to forming a habit you wish to establish, and do this faithfully for twenty-one days. By the fourth week, it should actually be harder *not* to engage in the new behavior than it is to continue doing it. According to Dr. Maltz, the key is that the twenty-one days need to be in a row. This is probably why your child (or mine, at least!) doesn't get into a good morning routine; weekend mornings are different from school mornings and are often routine-free.

Delegating tasks frees up your time and teaches children responsibility. The best routine for your child is the routine he or she helps establish with your help. You know your child better than anyone, so it's important for you to be the guardrails for your child's route. But let them choose their vehicle and their course.

In the beginning, your child's routine will be more like a daily to-do list. After several weeks, though, your child won't need the prompting that the written cues give. Some children will pick it up sooner than others; don't give up! Learning a routine is like learning to ride a bike; if mom or dad continues to hold on, the child doesn't learn balance.

23.   Create a Plan (and Avoid Whack-a-Mole Mom Syndrome)

Ever have a mommy meltdown? I'll bet it happened when you got away from your routine or didn't plan properly and, instead, turned into a Whack-a-Mole Mom, attacking (a.k.a. handling) things as they came up.

Let me give you an example: Last winter my oldest

son was diagnosed with food allergies. A lot of them. He had reactions to milk, casein, soy, eggs, wheat, rice, and corn, and we removed them from our diet. For me, this meant my five-minute meal plan all of a sudden didn't work, because the foods we normally ate weren't within the parameters of his new diet. And our once-a-week dinner out was out too, because until we knew more about the allergies, I wasn't going to trust restaurant chefs.

Unfortunately, cooking isn't my thing, and experimenting with recipes doesn't come easily to me. As a result, I tackled each meal as it came. I went to the grocery store almost every day, solving problems one at a time, Whack-a-Mole style.

With all of my time and energy spent struggling to find foods we could eat, everything else went by the wayside. If it wasn't on my immediate radar, I wasn't thinking about it. (That especially includes laundry.) So nothing got done. After a long week, I picked up my youngest son from school on Friday afternoon, came home and had a meltdown.

Lesson: Invest time in a plan. Use it. Don't become a Whack-a-Mole mom!

What's the difference between a routine and a plan? Remember, a routine is a "regular course of procedure; a habitual or mechanical performance of an established procedure." According to Merriam-Webster Dictionary, a plan is "the method used to achieving the end."

For example, your routine might be to make your grocery list on Monday afternoons. How you create your list—from a weekly pantry inventory review, the store circulars, or an emailed menu service—is your plan.

24. Create a Flow

Does your home have a good flow? A paper trail. A scheduling plan. Here's how it works in our house:

When my boys were little, I unpacked their backpacks with them and took out all of the papers to sort. Older children should be responsible for unpacking their backpacks and giving you all of the papers. Have a special place for this purpose: an area of your kitchen counter, an inbox, or a file folder.

I read all papers with my planner handy and make note of any special dates as well as special requirements (like he needs to bring a sack lunch).

Once I note the date in my planner, I file the paper for future reference. We have a countertop file box in our kitchen with file folders marked for each day of the week as well as one marked for schedules. I file the paper according to the day of the week the event occurs. I may or may not need to refer to that paper again, but sometimes questions arise about the event, and I like to have the written information at my fingertips.

Then I transfer the events from my planner to a schedule pad I have on our refrigerator. This pad is what keeps everyone else in the house in the loop.

Each night, before I go to bed, I glance at the schedule pad and check the next day's folder to see if anything special is occurring the next day or to make

Set Up a "Command Central" Station

Kate Hare is a busy mom of two girls who juggles family and work. Here is her story of setting up a command central:

> I started using leftover work binders to hold all those papers, such as school rosters, class rosters, reminders on snack policies, gym schedules, etc. I also learned (the hard way) to save old nursery school rosters for play dates with kids who now go to a different school.
>
> I use clear page protectors for the rosters and calendars, and pages with diagonal pockets to safely hold miscellaneous papers. The front inside cover has all our contact information (including favorite pizza delivery place and our address) for our babysitters. The notebook is a good central communication spot for papers that might otherwise get buried in my "in-box."
>
> On a big kitchen calendar I make notes for various appointments that need to be made. For example, when we come back from the dentist, I flip ahead five months to write a reminder note to make the next appointment. (I have found that if I wait until the postcard comes, it's often too late to get a timely appointment).

sure we turn in permission slips, order forms, or RSVPs on time.

25. Create a Mom Map

Molly Gold is the founder of Go Mom, Inc., and an expert in time management. She's also mom to three delightful children. She shares with us her secrets for family scheduling:

> My all-time favorite tip is color-coding your Mom Map. What do I mean? For time management that involves my family, I use a desk calendar that I actually hang on my wall. It's huge, has lines, and we color code it until its a piece of artwork every month. Each family member knows their color and is taught to check it daily and take charge of their own activities. It is the secret weapon in helping me get everyone where they need to be. Yes, I have to keep a separate calendar for myself, but that is part of my role as the gatekeeper of our family time. It's my job to work out the kinks, call in reserves, or simply call it a day when things just aren't going to work. By the time it's penned in marker on the Map, it's "gold!"

26. To Color Code or Not to Color Code: You Decide

I know of a lot of families like Molly's (see tip #25) who color code things to help with organization. Each child is typically assigned a special color, and activities for that child are marked in the calendar with his/her color of pen. At a glance, mom should recognize which activity is for which child because of the color. You can take this one step further and give your child towels, laundry baskets, toothbrushes, etc. all in his/her color.

Personally, I tried this approach but couldn't remember which son was which color … and I only have two children! It actually slowed me down, especially looking for my special colored pens. But if color coding sounds good to you, Alejandra Costello, founder of Color-Coded

Professional Organizing Services, shares her system for color coding a calendar:

> If you live a busy life, tracking appointments and events for yourself and your family can be challenging. When managing a schedule with children, try selecting a different color for each child. For example, Molly's dentist appointment and softball game should be marked on the calendar in pink while Peter's Boy Scout meeting and hiking trip should be marked on the calendar in blue. Color-coding the calendar is a fun way to ensure you never miss an important meeting or outing again.

Alejandra takes it one step further:

> Whether you're using a digital calendar or a daily planner, consider color-coding your schedule with the following color scheme:
>
> Red Marker—Appointments
> Blue Marker—Meetings, Children's Play Dates
> Green Marker—Events (Parties, Sports, Gatherings)
> Purple Marker—Holidays, Birthdays, Anniversaries, Occasions
> Orange Marker—Errands, To-Do List

27. Be Ready for Everything

Julie Morgenstern is a *New York Times* best-selling author, professional speaker, organizing expert, and corporate productivity consultant. Julie is renowned for an "inside-out" approach to problems and for generating customized solutions that are practical, insightful, and easy to maintain. You've probably seen her on *Oprah*, but did you know that she built her amazing business while being a single mom to daughter Jessi?

> Being organized, whether with your space or time, is all about being ready. It's about feeling in command so that you are prepared to handle all of the opportunities, distractions, and surprises life throws your way. We live in a complex, fast-paced world filled with infinite possibilities and opportunities. When you develop good time-management skills, instead of being overwhelmed by it all, you can celebrate it. You know what to choose. You feel clear and focused, ready to take on life.
>
> Less than two weeks before my daughter's Bat Mitzvah (a huge affair that, as a single parent, I had coordinated by myself), I got the call every author dreams of—it was from the *Oprah Winfrey* show. They wanted to fly me out to organize their offices as well as several viewers' homes for their big "Spring Clean-up" show . . . all within the next ten days!
>
> Was I ready to jump on this fantastic opportunity without hesitation? Was I organized enough to manage all of the details involved in pulling off both the Bat Mitzvah and the Oprah show simultaneously? The answer was a resounding yes! Because I was organized, most of the details regarding the Bat Mitzvah were done. What wasn't done was written on a list, and I could do a quick scan to see exactly where I stood. My planning and delegation skills came in very handy—I was able to prioritize the tasks and decide what my staff and friends could do in my place. My files and database were very organized, so any information I needed for either event was at my fingertips.

And during the whirlwind of the next two weeks, my planner kept me very focused on everything I had to do and every place I had to be. I didn't miss a beat.

My suitcase was packed in a flash and I was on the next plane to Chicago. Instead of missing the moment, I was able to embrace this unexpected convergence of priorities. The result was one of the most glorious weeks in my life—celebrating a momentous, spiritual occasion with my daughter, and appearing on the most coveted TV show in the world. Here's to the power of time management!

Here are some great time management tips for organizing your time as a parent:

- You have one life; you need one planner for all your activities. Select a single consistent planner, paper or electronic, that fits in your bag. Use it to record all work- and family-related appointments, activities, and to-do lists.
- Check your planner every evening to see what you accomplished during the day and what you have coming up over the next two to three days. Decide whether to carry over incomplete items to another day, or just let them go. Very few people ever get to everything on their to-do list.
- In planning your days, estimate the time required for each item on your to-do list. For example: Write thank you notes: thirty minutes. Run errands: one hour. Pay bills: one hour. This will keep your daily plan realistic and manageable.
- When writing appointments in your planner, be sure to write down the phone number, address, and directions next to the appointment in case you get lost or are running late.

28.   Hold Sunday Planning Sessions

Lorie Marrero is a certified professional organizer and the creator of ClutterDiet.com. She is also the mother of two teenage boys. Here's her recipe for maintaining her family calendar:

> We highly recommend Sunday evenings as a time when families can convene about the week ahead. Some families have a certain place they always go together in the car on Sundays, like to church or someone else's house for dinner. That is a great time to just grab your calendars before getting in the car and talk on the drive over. You don't have to call a formal family meeting unless you want to, but definitely go over these items once a week:
>
> - Review the calendar for everyone
> - Who is taking whom where, and when?
> - What evenings might one or both parents need to be out?
> - Is there a sitter required later in the week?
> - Who is in charge of homework help?
> - Who is cooking and doing dishes?
> - Who is doing bath and bedtime duty for younger children?
> - Who is doing cleaning and other chores?
>
> This simple ten minutes of planning will save you much confusion, embarrassment, time, and stress! Imagine knowing which nights you're responsible to cook and having exactly what you need, remembering in plenty of time that you need a sitter for Friday, and realizing that you need to switch driving for one day in the carpool schedule—without having to pull any last minute miracles!

Families might want to use columns for each person in the family, like "Joe, Sue, Bill, and Julie," and then write in their schedules below. I do this for my family's particular situation: "Notes, Driving AM, Driving PM, Breakfast, Dinner." You can customize this however you like, and experiment from week to week to find what works best. You could also create your own form in Word and print a new one whenever you like.

In business we talk about ROI, or Return on Investment, and the investment of a few minutes for this planning is a guaranteed ROI of your time.

29. Control Your Week

Nina Restieri is the founder of momAgenda and an organizing expert. She's also the mother of four children. Here's her advice on getting control of your calendar:

Spend thirty minutes of your weekend setting up your upcoming week in your day planner. I set aside time every Sunday afternoon or evening to plan out my week. With four kids at three different schools, and everyone doing different sports and after school activities, each day is like a carefully choreographed dance, with each step planned in advance. When I am finished with my Sunday night planning, I feel like I am in control of my week—and my life.

30. Don't Let Your Week Control You

We all know them. They're the moms who spend every afternoon in their cars shuttling kids from one activity to another. Maybe you're one of them. If you recognize this scenario a little too much, make a decision to unplug from overscheduled stress by capping the number of activities children can do at one time. Perhaps you allow one activity at a time—for example, hockey or baseball, but not both. Or maybe you allow one sports activity and another enrichment activity, such as Girl Scouts and soccer. When another recurring activity comes up, have your child choose to give up something or put the new activity on a waiting list.

Here's an interesting statistic: In a KidsPoll by KidsHealth.org, 90 percent of kids said they wish they had more time, 41 percent said they feel stressed out all or most of the time because they have too much to do, and 61 percent said they wish they had more free time.

Signs that your child might be overscheduled include: fatigue, anxiety, and/or depression; headaches and/or stomachaches; falling behind in schoolwork and/or dropping grades; trouble with friendships.

To help kids with balance, schedule at least one day a week on which kids have lots of free time. When your child has free time, so do you!

31. Schedule Me Time

In our quest to fit everything into a busy day, moms often try to save time by not spending any on themselves. Angela Jia Kim, founder of the organic skin care company Om Aroma, is also mom to a one-year-old daughter, Sienna Lucy Stedman. She shares a story about the day she gave birth to her daughter and the promise she made to herself:

I had to pinch myself in the middle of the night at the hospital . . . it felt like Christmas, only this was so much bigger. There she was in her own tiny little crib next to my hospital bed. My baby girl! I was so excited that I got out of the bed, my legs still wobbly and numb from the epidural, to get her and bring her into my bed. I just wanted to be next to her, hear her breathe, and make sure this was all real.

I couldn't wait to get home so we could introduce Sienna to our world. My instinct was to take care of her in every way possible, and I was completely consumed by her every cry and need. I could feel the shift of my world going from my husband and me to our baby.

I was about to leave the hospital when I remembered my vow: to take care of myself so that I could best take care of my daughter. The promise was to never lose myself and to take the time—even if it was just one minute—to make sure I was looking after my needs as well.

Ironically, my company had created a product line called the 1-Minute Ritual to Radiant Skin so that it would only take one minute for busy women to take care of their skin, breathe in beautiful aromas, and remember to center themselves. Even though I had the product, I had to force myself to take that minute for myself. It was an important moment, because, by taking that minute, I was fulfilling my promise to myself. And every morning, I remember to do it. It not only reminds me to get grounded and to breathe, it reminds me not to nudge myself out of the equation.

32. Make Your Mornings Ready for Broadcast

Face it: Mornings set the tone for the entire day. I can't tell you how many times I've put my boys on the school bus and breathed a sigh of relief. It sometimes feels like I ran a marathon and it's only 8 a.m.

When my oldest child was in preschool, our habit of stressful morning routines started. Before having children, I was always a night owl. I loved to stay up and watch late night TV. Conan O'Brien and I were pals. Our first son inherited my night owl ways and his sleeping habits mirrored mine. I worked from home and could set my own hours, so this arrangement didn't have any complications.

Enter preschool (a.k.a. complication). I actually had to get someone somewhere by a certain time. This made my freestyle method of mornings suddenly not so free. Adding to the degree of difficulty: preschool was just three days a week, so our "routine" wasn't a routine at all.

In addition to being a night owl, my son was also a deep sleeper. Waking him up wasn't pretty. I remember talking to some of the other moms, and everyone seemed to agree that mornings were hectic, that was just the way it was. I resigned myself to lots of huffing and puffing and hyperventilating until I made it to preschool . . . with my son . . . at 8:30 a.m.

Then my younger son was born, and we fired up the baby monitor. As moms know, sometimes baby monitors intercept other nearby baby monitors, and you can listen in on the goings-on in another household. And this is when I overheard my neighbor's morning routine. It was lovely. My neighbor was brushing her daughter's hair. They selected the right ribbons to use on her ponytail. They talked about what was planned for the day. Then the daughter said, "Mommy, can I brush your hair?"

"Sure, sweetie," she replied.

Oh, wow.

I was glued to the monitor. I smiled. My heart melted. I was filled up by the idyllic morning that was happening across the street.

Then terror struck as I realized: If I can hear what is going on at someone else's house, someone else can hear what is going on inside my house.

Oh, wow!

I started thinking about our typical morning. There certainly weren't any lovely exchanges going on. Just a lot of prodding, poking, and "hurry ups." I wouldn't want our morning routine broadcast on baby monitors across the neighborhood.

And then this thought entered my mind: If I don't want my neighbors to hear my routine, why on earth would I want my four-year-old son to be the recipient of it? The way I approach morning routines changed that day. They didn't necessarily become easier, but I made a decision to be purposeful about my time.

Would your mornings pass the baby monitor test? If not, what can you *Don't, Delegate,* or *Do* to change that?

33. Start Your Morning Routine at Night

The best mornings get started the night before. In fact,

what you do before you go to bed can make or break your morning. Mom of three Kim Meinen says:

> With a new baby and two preschoolers at home, our house can get kind of hectic. We have started laying out clothes the night before as well as setting the table with cereal in bowls with lids. Makes the morning go much more smoothly, especially if we need to get somewhere before noon!

Here are more ways you can wind down your evening to set your morning up for success:

Use a five- or seven-shelf hanging closet organizer labeled with the days of the week. Fill it on Sunday night and you're ready for the week. When your children are old enough, delegate this task to them. Be sure to select clothing items that your child can put on by themselves. Not only will this help you, but it will give little children a sense of accomplishment.

Make sure your child's backpack is packed for the next day and stored near the door. That means homework assignments, permission slips, lunch money, and nonperishable snacks are all in place, ready to go, eliminating last minute searching. Do not allow your children to finish homework in the morning, and be sure that any assignment or paper that needs your signature is signed before you go to bed. Again, when your child is old enough, he or she should pack his or her own backpack.

Lay out your own clothing for the next day. Make sure to iron any garment that is wrinkled or choose a wrinkle-free wardrobe. Make sure your clothing is not stained or damaged. Pack your briefcase or laptop bag and have it ready to go.

Pack lunches the night before. My boys check the school's lunch menu on Sunday and circle which days they will buy their lunch. To save even more time, I pack an entire week's lunches on Sunday night. The biggest trouble and mess in assembling a sandwich is getting the items out. I pack enough sandwiches for the entire week. Plain turkey or ham sandwiches pack ahead just fine, but you may not want to try this with peanut butter and jelly or sandwiches with condiments. You can also pre-pack items such as pretzels, carrot sticks, and grapes in plastic baggies or reusable containers. Then simply grab enough items for one lunch, place them inside your child's lunchbox, and put it in the refrigerator for the next day. Better yet, delegate the lunch packing to your child. In the morning, insert an icepack and put the lunchbox in their backpack.

Finally, get breakfast ready by stocking up on food children can serve themselves in the morning. When we stay at a hotel, my boys love the continental breakfast buffet. I think "continental breakfast buffet" really means "cold foods you can serve yourself," so I tell my boys that continental breakfast is served from 6:50 a.m. to 7:10 a.m. each morning and they can help themselves.

If you're a coffee drinker, set the coffee pot. Better yet, get one with an automatic timer so it's ready when you are, saving you a few minutes in the morning.

Check tomorrow's schedule. Make sure you have located and packed any items that are needed, such as a soccer uniform or dance leotard, library books, gym shoes, permission slip, school T-shirt or uniform, or completed project or presentation. When your child is old enough, delegate this responsibility to him/her.

And finally, check the weather forecast. Plan for rain, snow, or an unexpected cold front that might mean packing a jacket for your child to wear during recess. This is a good time to make sure the outfit your child has ready for the next day is appropriate.

34. Streamline Your Morning

Alarm. Snooze. Alarm. Snooze. Alarm. Snooze. Sound familiar?

In the morning, establishing and abiding by *your* routine is vital. Be sure to wake up before your child does so you can take a few minutes to "get your head in the game." Do you set your alarm a few (or several) minutes before you really need to get up and "snooze" for that extra time? You might be sabotaging your mornings! Sleep researchers say that those few extra minutes are not deep, restful sleep and may actually make you more tired as your day progresses.

35. What to Wear

You've heard the expression, "clothes make the man," (another gem from Mark Twain), but I believe clothes make the mom, too. A good outfit can affect your attitude. Too many moms feel throwing on whatever's clean or that old standby—jeans and an oversized T-shirt—is fine, but the truth is that when you look good, you often feel good.

I'll admit that spending time thinking about what to wear for a day at the (dusty) park or a trek to the grocery store often feels like time wasted. But whenever I feel lazy about my wardrobe, I remember one of my favorite quotes from Angela Jia Kim. After receiving a fashion makeover, complements of Tim Gunn's *Guide to Style,* she said: "Love your life enough to get dressed up for it." Wearing something that doesn't look like it could double for pajamas has affected my attitude.

Dana Wood, author of *Momover: The New Mom's Guide to Getting It Back Together (Even if You Never Had It in the First Place!),* has some tips on how to tackle the wardrobe challenge:

> Mentally plan your outfit while you're in the shower: Or at least think of the core jumping-off point to build around, i.e., a specific skirt, top, or pants.
>
> Stock up on dresses: Hands down, these are the best go-to pieces for getting out the door lickety split. Add a great necklace and hot shoes and you're off!

Jeans aren't bad. Just choose the right ones. Beauty expert Dimitri James says:

> It's better to own one or two pairs of great-fitting expensive jeans than many pairs of lesser quality. A great pair of expensive, well-fitting jeans can make a whole wardrobe!

36.   Shake Up Your Makeup Routine

You've chosen your clothes, now let's think about makeup. Dimitri James, who developed Skinn Cosmetics, has some advice for streamlining your makeup routine:

> First, stick to the "essentials": one great cleanser that removes makeup/eye makeup/mascara and leaves your skin feeling clean, and one great moisturizer with an SPF of at least 15. Use the cleanser with a cleansing brush or with a soft washcloth; it replaces the need for eye makeup removers, toners, and scrubs.
>
> Find a great bronzer gel, lotion, or powder and use it all over your face lightly, then heavier on cheeks and eyelids. This is a great substitute for makeup, eye shadow, and blush.
>
> A great mascara cannot be replaced! Just apply heavier and close to your lash base, and you won't need an eyeliner, or try smudging mascara along the lash line with the tip of the wand.

And *Momover* author Dana Wood chimes in here, too:

> Take your time with your makeup: Although it sounds counter-intuitive, taking a few extra minutes with concealer, foundation, blush, and eye makeup (liner, shadow, mascara) can actually save you time during the day because you won't be running to the bathroom for touch-ups. Likewise, applying lipstick with a lip brush rather than just swiping it on makes it last much longer.

37.   Say No to Bad Hair Days

Susanna Romano is co-owner of the high-end salon and

spa Salon AKS in New York City, and she has worked with celebrity moms like Sarah Michelle Gellar, Cindy Crawford, and Christy Turlington. Here's her tip for good hair days:

> Before you step into the shower, wrap your hair (doesn't have to be all of it) into Velcro rollers. Velcro rollers are a great time saver, because you don't need pins to secure them. This should take a matter of minutes. As you shower, simply keep your hair in the rollers. The steam from the shower will "set" your hair, giving you nice volume and wave. Once you are out of the shower, pull out the rollers and adjust. That's all it takes.

Dimitri James shares his hair tips:

> A slanted side part with a heavy side bang pulled into a ponytail is the freshest sophisticated easy hairstyle for a busy mom.
>
> Best to color your hair closest to your natural shade, maybe choosing a shade darker to brighten lighter skins or a shade lighter to brighten darker skins. Close to natural or a shade up or down will make re-growth more graceful and save on constant touch-ups. Avoid chunky or heavily highlighted hair unless you can "keep it up." There is nothing worse than hard re-growth.
>
> Find a hairstyle that respects the integrity of your hair! If you have curly hair, find a style that doesn't need to be worn straight in order to look good, and the opposite holds true for straight hair.

38.   Rise and Shine

If your child is a slow riser, add extra time into your schedule. Consider getting your child an alarm clock, making them at least partly responsible for getting up. If they miss their ride, they're at your mercy for a ride to school, or they will have to find another way of getting there. It's hard to let our children make mistakes, but one or two tardy slips might be all the motivation they need.

Set a time when everyone should be in the kitchen, allowing a few extra minutes for the unexpected, such as the baby spitting up on your clothes or the dog having an accident on the floor.

39.   Take Inventory of Your Mornings

Mom of two and owner of Style for Grace, a special occasion dress company for girls and women, Aimee LaLiberte, says family time is very important to her and her husband, Tom, so finding timely and efficient ways to better organize their household is crucial. She offers her solutions for getting out of the house on time:

> If you feel rushed with your current morning routine, and perhaps worse, you're departing five to ten minutes later than you want, you need to take inventory of your morning routine.
>
> For a week, I took inventory of how long it took me to do things I could do the night before: making the coffee (two minutes), filling water bottles (one minute), laying out the girls' clothes (four minutes), and determining if there were any baby essentials that needed replenishing and if so, placing those items in

the diaper bag (three minutes). When I realized that I could get ten minutes back by simply doing these tasks the evening before, I resolved my morning rush.

I also have taken an oath that on weekdays, I don't check e-mail or voice mail until I arrive at work. By reclaiming my morning routine, I find that the entire family feels less rushed and, most importantly, happier.

40. Create a Launch Pad

Do you (or your kids) waste time in the morning running around the house, gathering up all of the items for the day? Nina Restieri of momAgenda offers this tip:

> Designate one area in your house as the "launch pad" for school each day. This spot, which in my house is a small hallway off the kitchen, is where the kids leave their shoes, hang their coats, and leave their backpacks. If you have a mudroom, that would be a natural place for your launch pad. To get even more organized, set up separate bins, one for each member of your family, and teach your kids to use their bin for their shoes and backpacks and any other items. Implementing this concept in your house can be a big help in terms of keeping the rest of the house, especially the kitchen/family room area, neat and organized.

41. Make Mornings "Doable" by Instilling Some Don'ts

When I was in college, a girl on my dormitory floor had a sleep shirt that said, "I don't do mornings!" And she didn't: she scheduled all of her classes for 11 a.m. or later. While this approach worked for her, putting mornings on your *Don't* list certainly won't work for most parents. We must "do mornings," whether we like them or not.

That said, there are elements to your current morning routine that might go on your *Don't* list. For example, don't repair wardrobe malfunctions. Instead, choose something else to wear. Don't offer made-to-order hot breakfasts; make one entrée or stock up on self-serve choices like cereal or bagels. Don't turn on electronics. TVs, cell phones, video games, and computers slow people down. Make it a rule: use of any of these items is not permitted before you leave in the morning or, at the very least, until everyone is ready to leave and there is time to spare.

42. Have a Bedtime Routine

Bedtime routines are as important as morning routines. Professional nanny Michelle LaRowe, author of the *Nanny to the Rescue* book series, says having a consistent bedtime routine can help set your children up for a solid night's sleep. Once dinnertime is over, move on to the three Bs of a good bedtime routine.

1. **Bath.** A warm bath will help signal to your child's body that sleep time is near. A fresh diaper (or trip to the potty) will assure you that your child's toileting needs are met. Brush your child's teeth, offer a last sip of water, and head off to the bedroom.

2. **Books.** A few short stories can help settle your child down before lights out. Avoid adventure stories and instead choose soothing stories with a bedtime focus. Read the same number (no

more than three board books for toddlers) of books each night. For babies, follow book reading with a bottle and good burp.

3. **Bed.** A goodnight kiss, followed by an "I love you" is the perfect end to your child's day. Avoid prolonged and drawn out goodnights. Having a consistent phrase you say to each other before bedtime can help your child feel safe and secure. Place your baby in his crib when he is drowsy, but not yet asleep.

While it can be tempting to reenter the room once your child is tucked in, don't. Unless your child is ill or otherwise in distress, it's best to let them learn to soothe themselves to sleep.

43. Share Bedtime Duties

It might be tempting to always delegate bedtime duties to your spouse or partner. However, small children can be creatures of habit. If the same person tucks your child into bed every night, and then that person isn't home at bedtime one night, a meltdown can ensue. Whenever possible, share bedtime duties.

The Tools

When it comes to time management, every mom needs three basic tools: a planner, a wall calendar or schedule pad, and a filing center. But one size does not fit all when it comes to choosing the right items, so take some time and select the right tool for you.

Some moms prefer to use a planner as a portable office, complete with pockets, notepads, and a generous area to write. Others only need a small pop-in-your-pocket style, and for them, portability is the most important consideration. To determine which kind of planner is right for your organizational style, look at the calendars you already have. Chances are you have more than one style of agenda around the house right now. Which gets the most use? Did one start off strong, only to be abandoned in a drawer a few weeks later? Also, think about your personal style: how much and how big do you write? It's important to think of your planner as a portable tool, because many plans are made when you are away from home.

Once you understand your style and choose a planner, consider this your master schedule, the first place to record all of your events and activities.

To keep your family in the loop, post the schedule using a wall calendar, whiteboard, or schedule pad. Decide if you wish to see a week at a glance or the entire month. Choose a product that has enough space to record all of the activities of your family. And consider where you plan to post your schedule; does it need to be not only functional, but fashionable as well?

The final tool you need is a filing center, the place where you keep important information so that you can easily refer back to it for details when necessary. You have several options here: file boxes, file totes, filing cabinets, or binders. Decide which style works best for you. Do you want papers within reach? Consider a file box that you put on your kitchen counter or another convenient area. If you like to keep all papers together and have a home office, create a special section for family event information inside a filing cabinet. (That way you won't have to ask yourself, Did I file the lunch menu calendar under L for lunches or M for menu?) If you want to be able to take your files with you, portable file totes come in handy when you are waiting in the carpool line or at the orthodontist's office. If you want your papers out of sight but not out of mind, consider a binder with tabbed dividers that will allow you to easily organize papers and then stash it on the counter or away in a cabinet.

THREE
Chores and Simple Organization

44.   Create a Cleaning Routine

Like mornings and bedtimes, housekeeping is less stressful when there is a routine in place. Some jobs, such as making beds, loading and emptying the dishwasher, and feeding pets have to be done on a daily basis; some jobs, such as cleaning bathrooms, vacuuming, and dusting, are done weekly; and others, such as washing windows, wiping down baseboards, and cleaning closets, can be performed less frequently.

While many parents find it easier to tackle housekeeping alone, cleaning is a ritual in which children—even the youngest—should be included. Not only does getting the entire family involved make it easier on parents, participating in household chores can set the stage for success as a teen and young adult.

Dr. Martin Rossmann of the University of Minnesota found that the best predictor of a child's success is that they began helping with household chores between the ages of three and four. His study found that teens who had been given responsibilities as preschoolers were more likely to finish their education on time and have quality relationships. What's more, they were less likely to use drugs than children who started chores later or had no chores at all.

The key is to be consistent and make it easy for children to help. Routines are most easily followed when they are done daily. Be sure to give your children jobs that they should accomplish each day. For example, making their beds, picking up their toys before bedtime, and clearing their plates after dinner are three easy assignments for everyone in your household.

You'll also want your children to participate in larger tasks, things that are done less frequently. For example, each week your child can be responsible for dusting, emptying trash cans, or washing the bathroom sink.

Here are some ideas of chores you can assign to children of different ages.

Age 2 to 5

Pick up their toys and put them away

Help make bed

Sort through clothing, toys, and books for donations

Dust

Get the mail

Sort items for recycling

Clear plates from the table

Pick up sticks and leaves from the yard

Sweep the patio or porch

Age 6 to 10

Wipe cabinet fronts

Empty trash cans

Fold and put away laundry

Clean sink

Put away groceries

Feed pets

Help prepare meals

Set or clear table

Empty dishwasher

Help younger siblings with their jobs

Age 11 to 16

Vacuum

Mop

Scrub toilets

Walk pets

Prepare meals

Load dishwasher

Wash clothes

Iron

Clean out refrigerator

Make grocery list

Mow lawn

Take out trash

Neighborhood jobs such as babysitting, yard work, or
dog walking

Teens

Roll up rugs

File papers

Clean stove and oven

Wash windows

Wash cars

Grocery shopping

Deliver clothing to the dry cleaners or deliver donated
items to charity

Take younger siblings to sports practices or home from
school

Sample Routine

Leigh Caldwell is a travel writer known as Theme Park Mom. A busy mother of two, she has her family on a cleaning schedule. Here's her daily and weekly routine:

Everyone has a fifteen-minute job every day, such as cleaning one bathroom, dusting one room, or vacuuming one room. All the basics (floors, bathrooms, dusting) get done weekly this way, and I'm never left with hours' worth of cleaning to do on the weekends.

On the weekends, we all have thirty-minute jobs to tackle, which then get rotated and end up getting done once a month, such as dusting all the ceiling fans and light fixtures, cleaning out the fridge, and cleaning the garage.

45. Lower Your Standards

Faun Zarge is a mom to three children, ranging in age from four to nine, and she is also a trainer and speaker who specializes in helping women address their work-life challenges. She says one of the most frequently asked questions she gets is how to tackle housekeeping. Here's her best advice:

Lower your standards! Ask yourself if you would hold anyone to the same housekeeping standards you are keeping for yourself. The answer is almost always no.

Hire as much help as you can afford. Consider how much your time is worth and determine if it makes sense to pay for some house cleaning. Even if it isn't something you can afford on a regular basis, maybe it's something worth spending money on a few times a year, such as before the holidays or when company is coming.

46.   Prepare for a Project

Are you the kind of person who jumps into a project before thinking things through? You may be sabotaging your success. Molly Gold of Go Mom, Inc., shares this tip:

> The secret to completing home organization projects is estimating the time needed to do each project and then blocking that exact amount of time on your calendar. Sounds simple enough, but what is often overlooked is the planning that happens before the big day actually arrives.
>
> For example, if you are organizing your pantry that looks like a pack of wild animals ransack it daily, you will not only need to empty, edit, and replace items; you'll need storage solutions. Before you run to Target, assess what items might do well in a container, how many containers you might need for each category, and what size space you have to work in to determine that quantity. You'll also need to plan your shopping time. The key to getting this project done is taking the extra minutes to map out the steps and tools needed.

47.   Make Chores Fun

If you bark orders, you teach children that housekeeping is a punishment. If you talk about how much you hate cleaning, your children will hate cleaning, too. Instead, take a tip from Tom Sawyer and his white picket fence and make chores feel more like a game so you can get willing participants. Here are a few ideas:

- Set a timer and challenge your family to beat the clock. Everything seems fun when it's done as a time challenge. Use the timer to quickly sort clothes, clear the dinner plates, declutter a room, or put away groceries.

- Pull chores out of a jar or hat. Making it a game of chance means kids can't complain about the jobs they draw. Have one jar for daily chores and another for a weekly family chore day.

- Pair up. Everything is more fun when you have a partner to share it. Purchase two mops and have your children do the floors together. Separate the bathroom cleaning detail and give older kids who are always busy after school a chance to talk to each other while they scrub down the shower and wipe down the bathroom mirror.

- Play music. Upbeat songs make everyone move faster. Let your kids choose their favorite artist and dance while you vacuum, shake out the rugs, and do the dishes.

- Reward jobs well done with a special treat, such as a later bedtime, a favorite dessert, or an outing. Chuck E. Cheese offers a printable clean room chart at their website, chuckecheese.com. They even offer 10 free tokens for kids who bring in signed sheets.

48.   Rename Your Kids' Chores

I discovered a trick that has helped eliminate all of the reminding (a.k.a. nagging) I have been doing: I name chores something that sounds sweeter.

I know, I know. It sounds a little ridiculous, but it works! Here's what happened:

My boys, Christopher and Nick, have several chores they do during the week, most of which involve cleaning their rooms. Two chores, however, they seem to forget: bringing in the trash cans on trash day and filling the dogs' water dishes. I end up reminding them, which causes stress. So one night at dinner I started this conversation:

Me: "So, what did you do today to contribute to the family?"

Boys (in unison): "Huh?"

Me: "How did you contribute to the family today?"

Nick: "What does 'contribute to the family' mean?"

Me: "Good question. I'll answer that by telling you what I did today to contribute to the family: I prepared your breakfasts, packed your lunches, brought you to school, went to the grocery store, returned our library books, checked out a movie for family movie night, did a load of laundry, paid the bills, picked you up from school, and made dinner. All of those things helped the entire family, not just me. What did you do?"

My husband: "I went to work to earn a paycheck to pay the bills, I walked the dogs, I helped mom make dinner, and I will be coaching your hockey team tonight."

Me: "So, boys, what did you do to contribute to the family?"

Boys: (shrugged shoulders)

End of conversation.

The next night, I asked the same question. The results were pretty much the same, but I could tell that they realized that this question was going to be a part of dinner conversation. The third night, both boys sat down at the table with a different attitude. And this time, they got the conversation started.

Nick: "So, what did you do to contribute to the family?"

Christopher: "I gave the dogs water, I turned off the bathroom light that was left on, I brought in the paper, and I brought the laundry basket to the laundry room."

Nick: "Wow, that's great. I gave the dogs food, set the dinner table, let the dogs out, and helped mom make dinner."

Since we added this question to our dinner table conversation, I have not had to remind my boys to bring in the trash cans or give the dogs water. And they're finding ways to be helpful without being told. Calling a chore a *contribution* has put the task in context for them. How sweet is that?

49. Put Cleaning on the Calendar

Colleen McGee is a mom and stepmom. She tackled the special situation of delegating to a blended family by using her computer's calendar program. Here's how she did it:

When my husband and I married, we each had teens. A total of four lived with us at one time. To make things fair, I made a calendar on Outlook (Microsoft's time-management tool) of the tasks, scheduling recurring "appointments" for each person who did each chore.

For example, Sid had to share an upstairs bathroom with four people, so the cleaning of that bathroom was his chore every fifth time it came up for cleaning. Outlook let me choose to repeat the chore every fifth day. To keep it fair, I included my husband and myself on that list with chores we shared with the kids—like dishes and vacuuming a portion of the house. To make sure one person didn't end up with all the chores on one day, I rotated the start order for each chore listed for that day.

It was a little time intensive to set it up but it worked out pretty well. I would leave Sunday as a no chore day for everyone. Enforcing rules as a stepparent is tough enough. The list took the worst part out of it. It was the bad guy and not me!

50. Make the Most of Commercial Breaks

Alicia Rockmore is the co-founder of Buttoned Up Inc., an organizational lifestyle company dedicated to helping people get sanely organized. She, her husband Adam, and daughter Lucy like to take advantage of commercial breaks. Here's what they do:

> Once a week when the family is all together watching TV, take the time during the commercial breaks to tidy up the room. Give everyone a garbage bag for trash and things to be recycled. Have the kids put away toys, DVDs, computer stuff, even dirty dishes.

You will be amazed what a few people can accomplish in just two minutes and two seconds! In the course of an hour of *Extreme Home Makeover* or *American Idol,* the family room will be all together and Buttoned Up!

51.   Take a Picture—It Lasts Longer

Barbilee Hemmings is the mother of two girls as well as a retired schoolteacher and family coach. Through her company, Are You For Real?, she offers this great idea for helping your kids know how to keep your home clean:

> For busy families, "picture perfect" is the best way to stay organized. When the space is clean, take a picture and post it where you will see it. Now, every time you walk through that space, you will know immediately if something is out of order, and it will take you a quick minute to put it back in place. This is great for kids rooms, family areas, and kitchen cupboards.

52.   Write It Down

Kay Tomaszewski is a busy mom of two. She shares a delegating tip that works with teenagers:

> I have one tip that has worked very well with my teenagers. At this age they don't want to hear lectures and have "suggestive" hearing loss. I was wasting my time telling them over and over to do certain chores. Now I write down the chore on a piece of paper and also a time/day I expect it to be finished. Sometimes I write the note on a cute card with an "I love you" message. It works because they are SEEING what needs to be done instead of just hearing "blah

blah blah." And if I end up doing that chore, I take $1.00 off their allowance.

53. Use Rewards to Motivate Your Children

Using rewards to motivate children is controversial to some parents, and it's easy to confuse a reward with a bribe. But rewards are part of daily adult life. If you work at a job, you expect to be paid. Top-producing employees often earn bonuses. And when you stick to a weight-loss program, purchasing new clothing is a great reward.

You decide what's right for your household. Nancy Beck took a guilty pleasure—video games—and used it to create a reward system that has her children asking what chores they can do today. Here's her story:

> As a Christmas present when my son was about eight, I allowed his sister to buy him a video game console. I remember in my sleep on Christmas Eve I had an overwhelming feeling that I had just allowed something too powerful into my house. I was concerned that my children would become brain dead. Since my revelation came too late for my daughter to find a different gift, I had to have a plan.

Have a "Clean-Up Song"

Nina Restieri suggests: "If your kids are preschool age, try a "clean-up song." When my kids were that age, every time they heard the opening bars of "Here Comes the Sun" by the Beatles, they knew it was time to tidy up for a few minutes."

My children do chores around the house to earn video minutes. Any video/computer game that would not be found on the school's educational website requires video minutes to be spent. I then estimated how many minutes it would take to do a particular chore and that would be the amount of minutes earned. We sat down as a group and had a unanimous vote about the time payment.

For example, if sweeping the floor takes five minutes, then the person doing the chore gets five minutes of video time in his bank. We use a community jar of change on the kitchen counter. Each of my children has their own jar. As they earn minutes, they take change out of the community jar and place it in their own. And when they spend the minutes, they move them back into the community jar. The children keep track of their own time, and they tend to keep an eye on each other. They also have learned the concept of time in 60-minute intervals compared to money in 100-cent intervals. I have been satisfied with the results.

We also recently implemented video minutes as an incentive to perform better in school. Each time they score 100% on a school test, they earn an hour. For a score between 90% and 99%, they get half an hour. My son has been making better grades because of the extra hour he can earn.

I understand how much fun video gaming is for children. I watch them with their friends, and they really have a blast. I also know that there are a lot of downsides to gaming. So my thoughts are to allow it, but in moderation. With a clean house, there are only a limited amount of minutes to be earned and played in any given week. It has been a win-win situation for my family.

If you don't have a video game system in your household, is there another activity for which your child can earn minutes? Younger children might trade chores for play dates or trips to the park. Older kids could work for phone minutes or use of the car.

54. Rethink Your Chores

Renaming my boys' chores worked so well (see tip #48), I thought I'd try the same technique on myself. I started to think about the chores I do, especially the ones I'm not so fond of. Like meal planning. Oh, how I dread meal planning. I wondered if there was another way I could look at this chore to find joy in it. OK, maybe not joy. But could I find something about meal planning that would make me look at it differently?

I came up with a couple of ways to make the process better. First, I started asking my ten-year-old to help with the meal planning. The first time I asked him to help, he named his five favorite restaurants. Once he realized we weren't dining out, he dove into the task and started suggesting meals. And he's regularly on the lookout for new recipes (which cracks me up!) Two nights a week, my fifteen-year-old helps me with the cooking. Not only does he make my job easier, but we've started connecting in a way we hadn't before. While he's chopping celery and carrots for our salad, he'll discuss his day. I had heard that boys often talk more while they're engaged in an activity. It's definitely proven true with us.

Instead of thinking of this task as "meal planning,"

I've renamed it in my head "celebrating our family through food."

Which task causes you the most stress? Can you look at it in a new and interesting way? My mentor, Stephen Covey, says, "Begin with the end in mind." Can you channel the end result and rename it in your head?

55. Own Less, It's Less to Clean

Cut down on maintenance by cutting down on the volume of things that need to be cleaned. When my oldest son was about three, he loved his Little Tikes Car Mountain, which came with two cars. One yellow. One red. Each night before he went to bed, he counted his cars—one, two—and put them to sleep inside the car mountain.

My mother, who lived in another state, heard about his new favorite toy and how much he loved those cars, so she sent him several Matchbox cars to add to his collection.

Instead of being excited at getting more toys, he came to me, looking very worried. "I don't have time to play with all of these," he said.

Sure enough, instead of enjoying more, he saw the responsibility of owning more.

As my children got older and their collections grew, I noticed that the more of something they had, the less they took care of it. And I recognized this trait in myself. I had one nice nail file that was in my manicure set. I thought it would be nice to have more than just one nail file, so I purchased a few inexpensive emery boards and tucked them in drawers, here and there. It didn't take long before I could no longer find any of my nail files. Instead of putting them back where they belonged, I would put them wherever I happened to be. Yet ironically, when I had only one nail file, I always knew where it was, because I was careful to always put it back.

56. Find the Little Things That Make You Happy

Gretchen Rubin is author of the #1 *New York Times* best seller *The Happiness Project*. She's also a mom to two daughters. Here's one small thing she does to start her day:

> Make your bed! It takes almost no time or effort, but making your bed gives a real happiness boost. You start your day with an accomplishment (small, but real), you make your bedroom look more calm and inviting, and you demonstrate to yourself that you have control over the little things in your life—even when you don't have control over the big things.

57. Make Use of Double-Duty Tools

Having too many cleaning products can easily become counterproductive, making it hard for you to find the right tool. Instead, use double duty items. For example, put a dish sponge (the kind with the soap reservoir in the handle) near your child's bathtub, and put tile or dish soap inside. When they're finished with their bath, run it around the tub to avoid getting that dirty ring of soap scum. It takes just a minute, and it saves you time on bathroom cleaning day.

Choose all-purpose or multi-purpose cleaners to save time you might waste switching cleaners mid-job.

Although they are certainly convenient, disposable tools have to be replaced more often, adding time to your routine. Several years ago I discovered that the California Car Duster, which was made to dust cars so they didn't need to be washed as often, makes an amazing household duster. The strands of the big mop head are treated with paraffin, which traps dirt. Then you simply shake the duster outside to clean it. It can also be hand-washed in cold water. The large mop head makes dusting quick and easy, and it's more economical than using the disposable dusters that are meant to trap dirt. The company also sells a version to be used at home.

Leigh Caldwell is a busy mom who says she has little time for cleaning (and not enough money for a house-keeper!). She loves using microfiber cloths for cleaning everything.

> I buy my microfiber cleaning tools in the car wash aisle, where they are cheaper. My best find is a microfiber car wash pad on an extension handle, which I use to clean my showers and tubs. It covers a bigger area than a sponge, so it's much faster. And there's no bending to reach the bottom of the shower/tub.

58. Work While You Sleep

Remember when I said you could find five extra minutes in a surprising place: while you sleep? Well, here is what you are going to do with those found minutes.

- Clean your toilet bowl by pouring a cup of white vinegar in it before bed. In the morning, swish with

a toilet brush wand and you're set. You can also use
bleach and soak/sterilize the brush, too. I've also
heard that two denture tablets or a liter of cola do
the trick as well, but white vinegar is the most economical choice.

- Soak dirty dishes overnight, using dishwasher detergent (the kind you use in a dishwasher, not dish
soap) and hot water. This is often all it takes to turn
baked-on, caked-on messes into rinse-away jobs.

- Clean your microwave overnight by putting two
tablespoons baking soda and two cups of water or
three tablespoons lemon juice and three cups of
water into a microwave-safe bowl. Heat until the
mixture boils. Leave the door shut and let the liquid
sit overnight. The next morning, wipe down the
inside of the oven with a damp sponge.

- For dirty sinks, place a towel in the bottom of the
sink and cover with a bleach/water mixture. Let sit
overnight. In the morning, wipe down the sink with
the towel and rinse. Make sure you test your surface
to make sure it's bleach-friendly.

59. Work With Your Habits

Debbie Jordan is a mom and a professional organizer.
Through her company, VirtuallyOrganized.com, she
helps others realize the benefits of organization, simplic-
ity, and letting go of perfection. Here are her tips on tap-
ping into your personal style:

Sometimes the key to organizing success is simply a

change in habits. For example, if paper clutter is an issue, developing the habit of filing instead of piling can do wonders for your kitchen counters.

On the other hand, many times the reason that organizing attempts fail is that when we try to change our habits we simply meet too much resistance, either from ourselves or from the people we are trying to organize. In that case, we need to work with our habits rather than against them.

For example, if you find that you're always dragging your checkbook and bills out to the kitchen table, find a space in your kitchen where you can store a little basket for bills, your checkbook, stamps, envelopes, etc. Your efficiency will increase, and you'll be more likely to put everything back when you're done with this chore.

Analyze your habits and work with them rather than against them. Observe how your house looks on a daily basis. If you always lay your keys, mail, backpacks, etc. in a specific location, decide what piece of furniture would work to help avoid this pileup and make this space more functional.

60. Organize Your Home for Living

The key to cutting clutter in your house is to assign everything a home that matches *the way you live,* not the way you think would be perfect.

For example, if your family enters your home through a back door, laundry room, or mudroom, add storage nearby for shoes, backpacks, and coats. (They'll get dropped there anyway; you might as well make a nice home for them.)

Store your cleaning supplies in the rooms where they are used. You will be more likely to quickly wipe down a bathroom sink if the supplies are stored beneath it instead of in the kitchen or laundry room. Note: If you have small children who might get into your cleaning supplies, you will obviously want to store them out of reach.

When my son was a baby, I bathed him in the kitchen sink, and I kept shampoo, baby wash, towels, and washcloths in a basket beneath the sink.

If you like to curl up in the family room with a blanket and extra pillows, keep these items in a storage ottoman or entertainment center cabinet.

In addition to being easier to maintain, keeping items where they are used makes it easier for other members of your family to find things.

61.   Store Things Wisely

Store frequently used items front and center, so you don't have to waste time getting a stepladder each time you want to get it down. Use the high shelves for items used less frequently, such as holiday plates, spare silverware, or spare blankets.

62.   Tame Your Papers

In addition to schedules, permission slips, and birthday invitations, kids bring home plenty of "keepable" papers, such as artwork, pictures, and projects. Kelly Novotny is mom to a fourteen-year-old son and twelve-year-old daughter (and a very cute Cavalier King Charles named

Miley). Organizing is her passion, but she admits that sometimes life is too busy to organize pictures, report cards, and special projects. So here's what she does:

> I purchased a plastic file folder bin for each child and labeled hanging folders with each grade on a tab. As my kids brought special stuff home from school, I would file it. I also had two scrapbook type bins for each child. I would just place all professional school pictures (sports, communion, etc.) in each bin. Finally, last summer, I had the chance to make a school scrapbook album for each child. Everything was all in order when I had time to make the scrapbooks. The books are pretty amazing and each child has the same format with the same background but with a different life story.
>
> The most important part of this project was keeping things organized throughout the years. There was no time to work on the albums when my kids were younger, so having a place for each grade really worked for me.

63.   Make an Idea Archive

There is an article in a favorite magazine that you want to save. Instead of having a stack of magazines—all with articles you want to save—create your own personal archive or idea file.

Magazine subscriptions can pile up quickly, creating lots of clutter. Make a point of reading the issue when it comes in, and then recycle it or donate it to a senior center or women's shelter. But don't store it. If you are looking for information later, paging through magazine after magazine to find it will take up way too much time. Cut any articles you want to save out of the magazine or newspaper and create a binder to hold them. You can separate the binder according to topics or magazine titles. Better yet, many magazines post their articles online, so consider using the Internet as your alternative "personal archive."

64. Organize Kids' Rooms to Make Them Easy to Tidy Up

Have you ever walked into a messy garage or basement and turned around and walked out? Maybe you've seen those organization shows on television, such as *Clean Sweep* or *Hoarders,* and wondered how anyone could even begin to tackle such a mess.

Unfortunately, to a child, the chore of cleaning their room might feel exactly like that—an overwhelming mess. Today's children often have too many toys, too much clothing, and no good system for organization.

Start by taking a hard look at the items being stored in your child's room. Is there a better place to put some of them? Could the toys (or some of them, at least) be stored in a playroom or family room? Is the sports equipment better left in the garage? How many books, knick-knacks, and other items can fit on shelves?

You may be tempted to sort your child's belongings first, then purchase the right size storage bins. I take the opposite approach, which I call "Good and Plenty." When I'm organizing an area of my home, I select a "good"-looking storage bin in a size I consider "plenty" big. Choosing an attractive storage container will motivate your child to use it to put things away. It's also nice because it will be left out in the open, where it will be in constant view, but also where your child can easily use it. A good-looking container is less of an eyesore than an industrial plastic bin. Selecting the bin size before you fill it also allows you to objectively look at volume. If you have more items than the bin can hold, purge.

Most of us probably had a toy chest when we were children. Our children, however, seem to own more toys than we did, and an all-in-one storage spot for their toys just isn't practical (think of the digging and emptying of items it takes to find the Barbie at the bottom).

Help your child organize toys according to type and place them in bins (one for blocks, one for dolls, one for dinosaurs, etc.) Make it easy for children to put things away by labeling the bins, either with names or pictures for small children.

It's also helpful to give your children storage containers that are portable, such as bins on wheels or tote bags for toys (instead of heavy boxes). To make the most of your existing toy boxes, put canvas totes inside them, with handles that can be pulled out when your child wants to play with that item. This is helpful for toys and games that have small pieces.

When you give your child storage containers that are kid-friendly and reduce the amount of items that need to be cleaned, you are setting your child up for clean-room success!

65.   Make Your Child's Closet User-Friendly

One of the areas that seems to create the most trouble for kids is the closet. It can be like a black hole. To create a child-friendly closet, take a seat. Literally. Take a seat in front of your child's closet, and you'll see the dilemma from their vantage point. When it comes to organizing and storing your child's clothing, closets and drawers just aren't kid-friendly. Hanging items are hard to reach, and clothes kept in drawers are easily messed up or missed.

When it comes to closets, spare the rod and spoil the child by ditching hangers and using hanging closet organizers instead!

My youngest son, Nick, uses two hanging closet clothing organizers to store his sports uniforms, shirts, pants, hats, and sweaters. Each section is labeled (we have sections for school clothes, play clothes, long-sleeved shirts, short-sleeved shirts, etc.), so he can easily get dressed in the morning and put away his own clothes on laundry day.

The trick to keeping it neat is a trick that comes from expert suitcase packers: we roll his clothes instead of folding and stacking them. This is most helpful with his shirts; Nick can quickly identify each shirt and even pull one from the bottom without disrupting the shirts on top. Use this same trick with drawers: instead of stacking clothing vertically, place items inside as you would in a filing cabinet, rolling shirts and pants so children can see all of their items at one glance.

We use the closet rod to hang dress shirts as well as out-of-season clothing. And we have a small set of drawers inside his closet to hold socks, underwear, and pajamas.

If your child needs help selecting clothing in the morning, closet clothing organizers are perfect for organizing outfits for an entire school week. Simply assemble clothing for each day—everything from shirt to socks to underwear to hair accessories—and fill each of the five sections, making mornings easier. Choose an organizer with a decorative pattern, making that open closet door less of an eyesore. Store out-of-season items in bins on high shelves.

If you have upper and lower rods, use the lower rod to hang your child's everyday clothing and store out-of-season or not-the-right-size-yet clothing on the upper rod. Take a cue from retail stores, and use clothing dividers that you can label by clothing type, day of the week, or size (perfect for an infant's or toddler's closet).

You've Cleaned the Closet, Now What?

Each spring/summer and fall/winter season, purge your child's closet. Here are some websites where you can sell or swap your children's outgrown clothing:

Handmedowns.com   Ebay.com
Loobalee.com   Craigslist.org
Kidzola.com   Ebayclassifieds.com
Thredup.com

You can also sell clothing at Once Upon a Child or Plato's Closet (both of which are national consignment store chains) or look for a locally owned consignment store.

Store shoes in a hanging shoe organizer to keep them up and off the floor. You can utilize the floor space with bins for toys, bulky clothing, or dress-up clothes or to house a hamper for dirty clothes. I've found that when my children have an easy-to-use place to put their clothing and toys away, they keep their closets neat.

66. Organize the Backpack

Ashley Leeds and Alexandra Mayzler are the founders of Thinking Caps Tutoring in New York. They give tips for helping kids organize their backpacks.

When you take a look at your child's backpack, do you think, "How can he find anything in here?" Are you constantly missing newsletters and field trip forms? Let's face it: kids need help when it comes to organizing their backpacks. The backpack becomes a mess of torn homework and crushed paper airplanes. Here are a few simple tips to avoid backpack overload and paper avalanche.

Start fresh. You don't have to kick off a new organizational system when the school year begins. If halfway through the semester your child's backpack is a nightmare, clearly whatever method you're using hasn't proved effective. Help your child pick out new folders, notebooks, and binders: if he or she likes the materials, your child is more likely to keep them neat. Keep in mind: if your child brings home a lot of papers, a binder might be the most effective device, because papers don't fall out if it gets tipped over.

Sort, sort, sort. Now that you and your child have selected new folders, it's time to go through your child's mass of papers. Decide which papers your child needs for school, which ones can stay home (old projects and graded assignments belong in this pile), and which ones can go in the recycle bin (notes, doodles, duplicates). Create an at-home filing system for papers your child decides to keep so they don't get lost in the daily grind or take up backpack space, and sort current work by class so a math worksheet can be easily located. Don't forget to go through the pencil bag too, and throw out broken pencils and dried up pens: they take up space and your child doesn't need to play "third time's a charm" when looking for a writing utensil.

Check in on it. Once a week, take ten minutes to help your child go through folders and take out anything that is no longer needed for school and either recycle it or put it in the at-home file. By staying on top of folder clean-out, you avoid having to take an afternoon to clean out backpacks and desktops.

Keep a back-up supply. Now that the backpack has breathing room and the desktop has workspace, make sure your child has what he or she needs to get down to work: stock pencil bags with sharpened pencils, pens, erasers, a ruler, anything needed at school. At home, a desk drawer or filing box should be stocked with extra paper and supplies. Kids tend to get distracted when they don't have the materials at hand to complete assignments. By having everything in reach, the process should go smoothly (well, at least lack of supplies won't be the issue).

One thing to keep in mind when helping your child get organized for school is that it's an ongoing process: while you may devote a Saturday afternoon to backpack cleanout and school supply shopping, the process doesn't end there. If you don't make a point to keep binders and notebooks organized, your child's backpack can once again become a mess of wrinkled papers and misplaced homework. Think of backpack cleanout as a time to catch up with your child on how he or she is doing in each class, and get that bonding time that you may miss out on during a busy week.

67.   Lighten Your Own Load

Ever miss a phone call because you were digging through your handbag to find your phone? Or what about holding up the checkout line at the grocery store because you couldn't find your coupons? It might be time to purge your purse so you can cut down on searching time.

The first step to lightening your bag is choosing a smaller style. If a small bag just doesn't fit in your fashion radar, use your "evening bag mentality" and fill it with those things you need. Just because the purse is big doesn't mean it has to be filled to capacity.

Purge your bag routinely just as you would a closet. Take everything out of your purse and put it on the table. With each item, ask yourself these questions: Has this item been used during the past month? Does this item fit the needs of my daily tasks? Can this item be just as useful stored in my car or workplace? Am I carrying this item for someone else? If you answered no to either of the first two questions, then do not put this item back in your purse. If you answered yes to either of the second two questions, then these items need to be returned to their owner or stored somewhere else.

The glove box of your car is a great place to keep a small sewing kit, a pouch with medications such as aspirin or antacids, a compact umbrella, and an emergency snack to avoid drive-through temptation.

A full handbag isn't just messy; potential health risks come with toting around all that stuff. The American Chiropractic Association (ACA) recommends that a handbag weigh no more than 10 percent of its owner's body weight. Place your bag on your bathroom scale; you might be surprised at what it weighs.

68. Laundry: Reduce and Reuse

When it comes to trash day, your family probably already tries to reduce, reuse, and recycle. But what about laundry day? Busy moms can reduce their workload by establishing eco-friendly usage rules when it comes to clothing.

For example, how often should you use a bath towel before tossing it into the laundry? What about pajamas? Jeans? Sheets? I started looking at my boys' clothing before I washed it and found that many items were perfectly clean. I decided that I needed a prescription for laundry, so I made an appointment with the Clothing Doctor.

Steve Boorstein, better known as the Clothing Doctor, has written four books and created a DVD on the subject of caring for clothing and household fabric items. When it comes to bath towels, Steve asks two questions to determine how often they should be washed: What happens to the towel after it is used? And how good is the hygiene of the person using the towel?

Towels should be used and then properly hung to dry, meaning the towel is hung on a bar with air circulating around it. If it is tossed in a corner, a gym bag, or a basket, the bacteria on the towel will multiply, creating an odor.

Sometimes, especially in the case of children, towels also do the job of the bath or shower. In other words, while your child is in the shower or bath, do they use enough soap and shampoo to properly remove the dirt and bacteria from their body? If not, an increased amount of dirt and oils will transfer to the towel, which can cause odors.

Steve says he washes his personal bath towel every five days. With children who take shortcuts in the bath, he recommends using towels once or twice before washing. Once towels develop an odor, it can be hard to remove it, he says.

Moms might want to help children hang their towels after using them. He says the main problem with towels is odors. When washing towels, he recommends that you use enough detergent and don't overload the washer, so that towels can properly circulate, agitate, and rinse.

Sheets are similar to towels. How often you wash them is a matter of personal taste. If your child bathes every night before bed, you might wash sheets every two to three weeks. If not, washing sheets weekly is a good routine to get in. Steve also considers whether or not you eat in bed, and if you use lotions or face creams.

When it comes to clothing, like jeans or pajamas, Steve says it's a good idea to inspect the item to determine if it needs washing or not. For jeans that don't have noticeable stains, he suggests that you wash them after three to five wears.

69.   Laundry: Once a Week or Once a Day? You Decide

Five reasons to do laundry every day

1.   It becomes a routine and routines get done.
2.   You won't be overwhelmed by a mountain of laundry that will need to be done in one day.
3.   You can own less clothing because you wash more often.
4.   When you have less, you take care of items more.
5.   One load a day is just one load to fold and put away.

Five reasons to do laundry once a week

1.   The thought of doing laundry every day makes you feel like a hamster in a wheel.
2.   When you finish doing laundry once a week, you get a sense of accomplishment and something you can cross off of a to-do list.
3.   You can choose which day works best for your schedule.
4.   You can choose a day when your family is around and get more help with sorting, folding, and putting away.
5.   You are conserving water by making sure each load is a full load.

70.   Sort Your Laundry: Two ways

By Child, Not Color

> When doing laundry, rather than doing a load com-
> bined with the entire family's clothes, do a load per
> child (if you have enough and it makes sense energy-
> wise). It eliminates a lot of the sorting that has to
> happen when the laundry is being folded. And don't
> worry about separating dark and light clothes. With
> the exception of brand new or heavily dyed clothes, if
> you wash in cold water doing a mixed load will be just
> fine. —*Faun Zarge*

No, Sort Your Laundry By Color

> I use color-coded baskets for laundry. Like any other
> busy mom, I have a lot of laundry to do each week. I'm
> also really picky about how I sort clothes. So I have
> different baskets for each color. As I bring clothes
> down, I quickly sort them into each basket and make
> sure they're on the right side, clasps are hooked, etc.
> My girls like to help me do it—it's a great way for
> them to work on learning their colors. When a basket
> is full, I know it's time to wash that color. I can then
> just toss it into the washing machine.   —*Debra
> Spears-Turner*

71.   Use Mesh Bags in the Laundry

Mesh bags are designed to hold delicate items, such as
lingerie, in the wash so that they don't become stretched
or caught in your machine's agitator. But there are all
kinds of other uses for them. Here are two that are perfect for moms.

Put your do-not-dry items in a mesh bag so that you

won't accidentally throw them in the dryer. I can't tell you how often I pull a pair of jeans or sweater out of the dryer because I forgot to separate it and air dry it.

Assign each member of your family a mesh bag to hold their dirty socks. This will eliminate the time it takes to match socks by keeping each person's socks together during washing and drying.

72. Label Your Kids' Clothing (So You Can Tell Whose Is Whose at a Glance)

Throw the laundry in a basket and it all looks alike. If you have children close in age, sometimes folding and sorting clothes can be a "CSI" moment. "Is this white sock Logan's or Mitchell's? Let's send it to the lab for DNA testing."

You could pile all of the clean clothes in the center of the room and yell, "Come and get it!" But I'm not sure that would be any easier.

Or you could color code your kids' clothes by assigning children different colors and marking each item with a dot in that color. But who can remember which color belongs to which child? Who can keep track of all those Sharpies? How do you handle the hand-me-down issue . . . can you cover a blue mark with a yellow marker? And what are you supposed to do when Grace announces that she is *not* green, she is fuchsia!

So how do you quickly sort and fold the laundry?

The solution came to me while watching an old Charlie Chan movie. Charlie refers to his oldest as Number One Son. Lightbulb moment: What if I put one small

Assemble a Handy-Mom Toolbox

Imagine if the plumber had to go look for his wrench every time he arrived at a job. Seems a little silly, huh? But we moms can waste a lot of time looking for items we use (nearly) every day. If you find yourself searching for the same item more than once a week consider creating a handy-mom toolbox.

Here are nine household items that can make a mom's life easier. Keep them handy:

1. **Timer.** Sure, timers time dinner. But they can do so much more than that. Time a study or reading session. Play beat the clock, and turn chores into a game. Sharing toys becomes fair when each child gets the same amount of playtime. Time timeouts. Cut down on long phone calls (this works for both you and your tween).

2. **Dry-erase marker.** Moments of inspiration can come at any time, even when you are washing your face or brushing your teeth. Keep a dry-erase marker in the bathroom drawer to jot down on the bathroom mirror whatever it is you want to remember. You can also use this technique to leave messages for your husband or children or list your errands on your car windshield (but please, don't make notes while your vehicle is moving!!!).

3. **Permanent marker** (such as a Sharpie). If the lost and found is your child's closet away from home, label his or her coat and lunch box with a Sharpie. Sorting the laundry can be like playing detective. Does this sock belong to your oldest or your youngest? Use a Sharpie to label clothing tags or socks at the toe to cut down on the confusion. Label your frozen food. You might think you can tell the difference between ground beef and stew meat, but when it's frozen inside a Ziploc bag, it all looks the same. Use a Sharpie to identify contents and dates.

4. **Ziploc bags.** Speaking of Ziplocs, moms need lots of them. They're perfect for holding dirty clothing, wet bathing suits, or a clean change of clothes. Use one to store little pieces of games, puzzles, or toys. Fill a Ziploc with toys to take to a restaurant, Grandma's, or church, keeping young kids busy. An empty Ziploc is perfect for storing a snack on the road or holding your child's unfinished lunch or dinner. Ziplocs are perfect for holding items that might leak inside your suitcase, diaper bag, or purse. Big Ziploc bags are great for holding muddy soccer cleats or sports uniforms, so they don't mess up your car. Ziplocs can also make great ice packs . . . or pastry bags!

5. **Rubber gloves.** Sure, you can wear them to scrub a toilet or wash the car, but did you know they can also remove pet hair? Dip into cold water and shake off the excess. Then run your hand over furniture and clothing. Pet hair will collect on your glove. Rubber gloves are also great for opening jars and can also help you hold slippery items, such as the buttered Thanksgiving turkey, moving it from the sink to the roasting pan or roasting pan to platter. Weeds can be stubborn, but rubber gloves give you a good hold when pulling the tough ones out of your flower beds. Rubber gloves are also perfect for sorting your recycling. And they can help you get out of (or into!) a tight spot. Use a pair to pull on tight bed sheets or pull up delicate panty hose without worrying about poking a hole with your fingernail.

6. **Rubber bands.** Remember MacGyver? He was always able to get out of dangerous situations using seemingly mundane tools. Such as a rubber band. Moms can use this handy tool for lots of uses, too. Baby-proof cabinet doors by hooking a rubber band around the knobs. Use a rubber band as a bookmark. Put a rubber band around the end of a spoon to prevent it from falling into the bowl or pan. Put one on a pump soap

dispenser to save soap. Put one on your thumb to easily work through a stack of papers. Or put one around your car visor to hold papers until you get home. And pregnant moms know that a rubber band can prolong the life of your pants (and keep you out of maternity wear) by holding your top button closed.

7. **Paper clip.** A survey by Lloyds of London found that only 20 percent of paper clips are actually used to hold papers together. The other 80 percent? Well, they are used as chip clips, bookmarks, ornament hangers, and hitting the reset button on your electronic device. Moms also can use a paper clip to unclog the glue bottle or scrape grout. Paper clips can be an emergency diaper pin, hem repair, or even a way to fix a broken button or broken glasses. Use paper clips as counters when teaching your child math. You can also give a paper clip to a bored child and see what kind of shapes they can create. Or create a paper clip chain and hang your child's artwork.

8. **Sticky notes.** Sure, they're great for posting a quick note or phone message to a family member. But sticky notes are also great dividers when organizing a stack of papers. They are also great bookmarks or flags for recalling important information. Put a pad in your car so you can leave a note for someone who wasn't home when you stopped by. Or leave yourself—or your children—reminders on the bathroom mirror or on the back door.

9. **Paper towels.** Of course, paper towels are great for wiping spills. But they also make useful napkins. You can blot grease from burgers, fries, bacon, or other homemade foods. Make your own baby wipes (you can find "recipes" online). Keep a roll in the car for whenever the need arises.

dot on clothing and items belonging to my oldest (a.k.a. Number One Son) and two dots on clothing and items belonging to my youngest. Adding a second dot easily solves the hand-me-down issue, and I can use any color ink I desire.

The best part? I can easily identify which son left his socks on the bathroom floor. (Spoiler alert: It's usually Number One Son.) As Charlie Chan says, "Small things sometimes tell large story."

73. Just Say No to Ironing

Jennifer Tankersley is a busy mom to three children and founder of ListPlanIt.com, a website that offers hundreds of premade lists for busy families. Jennifer is an expert at ironing out details, but she doesn't care much for ironing out wrinkles. Here's what she does to avoid ironing day:

> I don't want to iron my family's clothes, so I fold my clothes directly out of the dryer. This not only keeps them from getting wrinkled when they are thrown into a laundry basket and sit for possibly a day (or two), but it saves me a step later on.

FOUR
Meals and Groceries

74. Create a Weekly Meal Plan

I used to daydream that I was married to Jerry Seinfeld. Not because he's funny, or even because he's famous. No, it was because Jerry seems to embrace cereal as a culinary dining option.

Oh, I could just imagine it:

> **Me:** Here is your dinner, honey: a delicious bowl of Grape Nuts!
>
> **Jerry:** What is the deal with Grape Nuts? You open the box—
>
> **Me:** I know, dear, "no grapes, no nuts." So do you want skim or 1 percent?

Alas, I didn't marry Jerry. I married a nice Italian boy whose nice Italian mom can cook up a storm. And meal planning isn't my thing. So, every day around 6:00 p.m., I used to have a little bit of a panic attack.

And I wasn't alone: 37 percent of families admit that they don't know what they're having for dinner until they start cooking. This is like loading your family in the car for an outing and having no idea where you're going until you start driving. Do you know how to get there? Do you have enough gas? Will everyone enjoy the destination? This situation can cause stress and frustration.

If deciding what to have for dinner is a task that causes you stress, too, consider creating a weekly meal plan. It can be as involved or as simple as you want. We've adopted a super-easy, five-minute meal plan: we eat the same dish on the same night every week. Before you roll your eyes and chant BORING!, humor me. This is my family's meal plan, and here's why: I don't enjoy cooking, and my family is more meat and potatoes than gourmet cuisine—they prefer the predictable.

Our week goes like this: On Mondays we have Mexican, Tuesday it's chicken in the crock pot, Wednesdays we have soup and sandwiches (soup and salad in the summer), Thursdays we have pasta, Fridays we have pizza, Saturdays we grill, and on Sundays we have Sunday dinner.

The key to making this work is having some tried-and-trusted alternatives in your arsenal to break out when boredom begins to set in. For example, Sunday's standard dish is spaghetti and meatballs (it was a tradition that my Nana started). But every so often I make a turkey or a roast. Monday's no-brainer dish is beef tacos. But occasionally, I'll make quesadillas or fajitas. Most Tuesdays, we have chicken in the crock-pot over rice, but sometimes I make chicken and dumplings. You get the idea. The standard meals create a standard grocery list and a standard item to take out of the freezer each night, which makes meal planning almost a no-brainer.

75. Skip the Meal Plan and Play Pantry Roulette

There is one thing I have never taught my body how to do, and that is to figure out at 6 a.m. what it wants to eat at 6 p.m.

—ERMA BOMBECK

Perhaps you feel this same way. Staring into a pantry can be a fun challenge for some people. If you get stumped, you can turn to sites like recipematcher.com, super-cook.com, myrecipes.com, or recipepuppy.com, all of which allow you to enter whatever random ingredients you have on hand and get suggested recipes.

76. Use a Meal-Planning Service

Sometimes it's not the *cooking* that makes mealtime difficult, it's *deciding what to cook*. If this is the case for you, consider signing up for a meal-planning service in which a menu plan, corresponding recipes, and a grocery list are delivered to your email inbox each week.

There are several fee-based meal-planning services available, and each has its strengths. You can access sample menus at each website, so be sure to try before you buy.

The Six O'Clock Scramble (www.thescramble.com) offers family-friendly healthy meals with corresponding grocery lists. Founder Aviva Goldfarb has written two cookbooks, and her specialty is creating meals that contain whole grains, seasonal items, less-processed ingredients, and lower fat. Each meal contains a full nutritional analysis.

E-mealz.com is a customized meal-planning service. Members can choose from several plans, including low-carb, points systems, vegetarian, and plans that match the menu to what's on sale at your favorite grocery store. The plan includes recipes as well as a corresponding grocery list.

Dinewithoutwhine.com and Dinnerplanner.com are two meal-planning services that cater to families with small children.

Free meal plans are available at Monthlymenuplanner.com. You can also visit Organizing Junkie's website at

Orgjunkie.com, where she posts her Menu Plan Monday. You can peruse other families' meal plans. Or grab a copy of *Woman's Day* magazine and take advantage of the month of meals they plan for you. You can find the menus at Womansday.com under the Recipes tab. Click on Month of Menus, which brings up the menus with printable grocery lists that correspond with the week's meals.

77.   Engage the Family in Meal Planning

Since everyone eats, ask everyone in your home to make a list of favorite entrées and side dishes, including soups, salads, potatoes, pasta, and vegetables. Write each dish on an index card and combine the cards to create a meal for each night of the week.

78.   Go High Tech

Barbilee Hemmings of Are You For Real suggests:

> Make a list of everything your family likes to eat, from eggs and toast to a five-course meal to eating out. Separate each item into categories, such as Breakfast, Lunch, and Dinner. Using a simple table (programs such as Microsoft Word or Excel can set them up), create as many menus as possible from the foods that you like to eat. Every Sunday (or whatever day you choose) pull out a menu, make your grocery list, and voila! You have your weekly meal plan.

Plantoeat.com is a fee-based website that creates a spreadsheet for you. It allows you to enter recipes or import them from websites or blogs. Then you drag recipes from your virtual recipe box to your week. It coordinates your grocery list, too. You can sign up for a free 30-day trial membership. If your child or partner is tech-savvy, this might be a good task to delegate.

79.   Always Think Ahead

Erin Chase is author of *The $5 Dinner Mom Cookbook* and mom to three little boys. She loves couponing, grocery shopping, and planning affordable—very affordable— dinners! Here's her advice on how to stay on top of meal planning:

> Ask your family members what new meal they would like to try, and incorporate it into the next week's or next month's meal plan.
>
> Keep a notebook or bookmark all recipes that you come across that you'd like to try. When it comes time to plan your meals and you draw a blank, you've got a notebook full of ideas!
>
> Always be thinking about the next snack or meal. When the kids are finishing up breakfast, be thinking about lunch or afternoon snack. Just before the kids come home from school, pull out what you need to make dinner and chop an onion or dice a tomato while you have a second. If you work outside the home all day, survey the fridge and pantry the night before and pull out the necessary ingredients for the next day's meals.

80.   Do Your Meal Planning with Friends

Make meal planning fun by combining the mundane chore with a girls' night out. You can simply bring recipes and your calendar and swap meal ideas, penciling them in together. Consider creating a Facebook group, blog, or other online community for your recipe friends where you can post feedback.

Or make it more of an adventure by visiting a meal preparation kitchen such as Dream Dinners or Super Suppers. You'll leave with a week's worth of meals ready to go into your freezer. It's not necessarily budget-friendly, but with a group of friends, it's definitely fun.

Alternatively, you can easily try this same concept at someone's home. Gather four of your friends and have each person bring the ingredients for their favorite dinner recipe, enough to serve each friend's family. Then have a large cook/assemble party. Each person will leave with enough meals for a week. Be sure to package the meals so they can be frozen. And check out HotBy6.com, a cool fee-based website that offers meal plans for pre-assembled freezable meals.

You can also organize an ongoing meal swap co-op. Gather four friends (for a total of five including you) and ask each to cook a meal, making enough for five families. Swap meals and you've got your meals planned for a week.

81.   Have a Go-To Meal

Always have a go-to dinner in the freezer for nights that just don't go as planned or when you just don't feel like cooking. For me, it's Trader Joe's Fried Rice, to which I add my own chicken. This cooks up quick, and my fam-

Pantry Staples

Tracy Alt is a professional organizer and founder of the website Tips-to-Organize-Life.com. She created a family-friendly pantry staples list. Take a look:

> Stocking up on often-used pantry items when they are on sale is the perfect way to not only save money on items you know will not go to waste but also to ensure that you will have enough ingredients on hand at all times to throw a meal together in a matter of minutes. Here is a list of my top ten pantry items that will help you add that all-day cooked flavor to quick-cooking meals.

> 1. **Pasta:** Pasta is so versatile that you could make dinner with it every night for a month and never have the same meal twice. Dried pasta is the perfect pantry staple to stock up on every time it goes on sale at your grocery store. Keep different sized and shaped noodles on hand to make meals more interesting. Dried pasta can be added to soups, stews, or casseroles, it can be used as a bed for your favorite stir-fry, to add some bulk to your meal, or it can be the star of the show—a quick go-to meal made by simply adding your favorite jarred sauce. A couple of things to keep in mind when cooking with dried pasta: Always put your pot of pasta water on the stove before you do anything else to begin preparing your meal. You don't want to have the rest of your meal prepared and getting cold while you are still waiting for the pasta water to boil, so give it a head start. Also, if you are serving pasta as the star of the show, topped with your favorite sauce, you should always use a noodle with lines or ridges in it, because it will give the sauce a place to go; also,

do not rinse the noodles when you drain them because it will help the sauce stick.

2. **Spaghetti Sauce:** Of course you can use a jar of spaghetti sauce to pour over spaghetti for a quick meal any night of the week, but think outside the box a little when it comes to this pantry staple. You would be surprised how many different ways spaghetti sauce can be used. The great thing about spaghetti sauce is that all of the cooking has been done and that all-day flavor is already sealed in. There are so many varieties on the store shelves that you can get a sauce with whatever flavor combination you prefer, or you can get a simple marinara sauce and spice it up your own way by adding fresh herbs and vegetables to suit your palate and your menu.

3. **Prepared Broths:** Boxes or cans of prepared beef, chicken, and vegetable broth are a must-have pantry staple. When it comes to quick cooking, you should not pass up any opportunity to add flavor. You can do this by substituting broth in place of water to add extra flavor to any recipe. You can even cook your rice in broth instead of water. The larger boxes of broth can be stored in the refrigerator after opening, so if you cook often, you can use as much or as little as you need. They can sometimes be a better bargain than the cans. If you do wind up with leftover broth in an opened container and are afraid that you will not be able to use it quickly, pour it into ice cube trays and freeze it. You can pop out as many cubes as you need and melt them right into your recipe. You can even get fancy by adding some dried herbs to your broth cubes before freezing for extra flavor.

4. **Quick-Cooking Rice:** Rice is a great way to add bulk to a meal. Serving a stir-fry of meat and veg-

etables over rice makes a delicious and satisfying meal. Using brown rice or wild rice instead of white rice is also a great way to add some whole grains to your diet. Experiment with different flavors and find one that your family enjoys. Rice also makes a great side dish either by itself, with vegetables mixed in, or simply topped with your favorite spaghetti sauce.

5. **Condensed Soups:** Condensed soups are a fabulous way to add both moisture and flavor to quick-cooking meals. You will find recipe ideas right on the soup can labels, and there are entire cookbooks written around the theme of cooking with condensed soups. Cream of mushroom, cream of chicken, cream of celery, and condensed cheese soup are probably the most popular. Take a close look at the soup selection the next time you are in the grocery store. Read the recipes on the labels and stock up on any that you can incorporate into your weekly menu planning. If nothing else, you can make soup for lunch or dinner on a cold and rainy day. Don't forget the chicken noodle in case somebody doesn't feel well.

6. **Dried Herbs and Spices:** Having a stock of herbs and spices on hand will really help "spice up" your quick meals. Kosher salt, whole black peppercorns (to grind in a pepper grinder), parsley, basil, oregano, rosemary, thyme, cumin, chili powder, mustard powder, and paprika are a great starting point. Unless you cook a lot, buy these items in the smallest quantity possible. Dried herbs and spices lose their flavor over time and should be replaced after 6 months. You will wind up wasting money if you buy the jumbo size container of paprika, only to use it once or twice and have to throw it away.

7. **Liquid Condiments:** Worcestershire, soy sauce, hot pepper sauce, and an assortment of vinegars are some liquid condiments that can pack a punch when it comes to adding flavor to your quick-fix meals.

8. **Canned Tomatoes:** Having a variety of canned tomato products in your pantry is a great way to add all-day cooked flavor to your meals. You can add variety by mixing up the size of the tomatoes, from whole to finely diced. You can even purchase cans with herbs and spices already added.

9. **Canned Beans:** Beans are a great source of fiber and an excellent way to add bulk to your meals, but cooking with dried beans can take a very long time, because you typically have to soak them overnight and then cook them for hours until they soften. Canned beans give you the same benefits in a fraction of the time, and if you stock up when they are bargain-priced, they can be beneficial to your wallet as well.

10. **Extra Virgin Olive Oil:** Extra virgin olive oil is an absolute cooking staple. Even though oil is a fat, extra virgin olive oil is considered a healthy fat. It contains antioxidants like Vitamin E, it can lower your bad cholesterol while raising your good cholesterol, and studies have shown that extra virgin olive oil can actually help prevent heart disease and certain types of cancer. You should keep in mind, though, that even with all of these health benefits, extra virgin olive oil is still a fat and it should be consumed in moderation. Two tablespoons per day should be your limit. There are many varieties of extra virgin olive oil on the market, and some can be very expensive. Do a little taste testing to find a moderately priced brand that suits your palate, and watch for it to go on sale.

ily loves it. I stock up and always have a few extra bags in my freezer. My family also enjoys Costco's Kirkland brand lasagna. It tastes close to homemade!

Is there a brand of frozen food that your family loves? What about jarred spaghetti sauce? Stock up on these items so that you can turn them into your go-to meal.

82. Schedule a Night Off for the Cook

In 89 percent of households, the mom prepares breakfast, lunch, and dinner seven days a week. That's twenty-one meals to think about every week. When planning meals, close your kitchen one night. You can dine out, order carry out, or call it leftover surprise. You can also delegate the meal planning and preparation to another member of your family at least once a week.

Any task you have to do every day will become a task that you eventually need a break from. Be sure to plan a mini-vacation from cooking at least once a week.

83. Plan Ahead When Eating Out With Kids

Nothing ruins a dinner out faster than bored and hungry children—for you and anyone seated near you. ClubEtiquette.com founder Gigi Lewis says parents should do a little prep work before taking children to a restaurant.

"My mother always told me what you do at home, you will do away from home," says Gigi. "Today, I believe this more than ever. If you and the rest of your family show respect and traditional courtesies at the table at home, it will transfer when you are in a public dining setting."

This means if your children are allowed to fidget, run around, eat with their fingers, and play with their food at home, this is the behavior you will see when you eat out. Don't assume your children will magically follow different rules when they are at a restaurant.

Gigi suggests that families role play at home. "Actually sitting down together as a family for a meal gives several opportunities to teach proper dining behavior before you are ever in a restaurant," she says.

Before going out, explain to your children what type of behavior you expect. Set some ground rules and be sure everyone knows what behavior is acceptable and what is not. Then, remind them of the rules before entering the restaurant.

"If you know that little Jake has issues with keeping his napkin on his lap during the meal, gently remind him of that one rule before entering the restaurant," Gigi says. "Working on one rule at a time is sometimes just more manageable and effective for the parent."

Smart parents set up the dining-out experience for success by choosing family-friendly restaurants. It's also a good idea to bring along a bag of tricks. Most restaurants have kids' menus that feature games. But packing a bag with books, games, and art supplies is a good idea in case the wait for food is longer than expected.

Young children might have a hard time waiting for the food. It's a good idea to pack healthy treats, too, to calm grumbly tummies.

Eric Muller wrote a great book called *While You're Waiting for the Food to Come,* which gives families experiments and games to do with items you find on a typical restaurant table. The book is out of print (check your local library or used book store), but you can print out some of his experiments at the website Doscience.com.

The most important thing to remember when you dine out is to respect the others dining around you. It's very likely that someone seated nearby is paying a babysitter to watch their children. The last thing they should have to deal with is someone else's misbehaving kids.

84.   The Grocery Store: Choose Your Moment Wisely

According to the Time Use Institute (TimeUse-Institute.org), every day 32 million American adults shop at a grocery store—one out of every seven adults nationwide. Women account for two-thirds of all grocery shoppers. Saturday is the busiest grocery shopping day, followed by Friday and Sunday. The least busy days are Monday and Tuesday. On weekdays, the highest traffic in grocery stores is between 4:00 and 5:00 p.m., suggesting that people are stopping at the grocery store on their way home from work. On weekends, peak shopping times are between 11 a.m. and late afternoon. The average time spent in a grocery store during a single visit is forty-one minutes, and women take longer to shop than men.

Armed with this information, plan your shopping for Tuesday mornings. Mondays may be less crowded too, but grocery store staff is often busy restocking shelves and produce on Monday.

85.   Make a Shopping List and Stick to It

We all know that you shouldn't go to the grocery store hungry. You also shouldn't go to the grocery store without a list. A list will help you avoid impulse buys as well as forgotten items and second (or third!) trips to the store each week.

If you have a coupon for one of your items, attach it to your list with a paper clip or highlight it on your list so you don't forget.

If sitting down to write a list is too time consuming, check out MyGroceryChecklist.com, where you can check items off on your computer, click a box, and create a printable list. Another site that will help you create a list is GroceryWiz.com. This site also matches up available online coupons to your list. And yet another site, Aislebyaisle.com, allows you to create a list that corresponds to the layout of your grocery store.

Making a list doesn't just save you time. CNN recently reported that the average shopper spends between $0.50 and $1 for every minute they spend inside a grocery store. Get in, get out, save money!

Elizabeth Goodsell is a busy mom and the founder of That's Neat! Organizing in Boston. Here is her tip for how your computer can help with your grocery shopping:

> To make grocery shopping easier, use your computer to create and print a list of the items you buy regularly. Organize it by aisles or sections, such as Produce, Deli, Meats, Baking, and Snacks. You can use an aisle map from the store (available at the Customer Service desk) to help put items in the right aisle on

your master list. Keep your list on the fridge and
check off what you need. When you go to the store,
your items will be grouped by the right aisle, saving
you time in the store.

Finally, grocery lists can also be entertaining. Check
out GroceryLists.org. The site offers what it calls the
"Ultimatest Grocery List." But you also must visit the
quirky website Bill Keaggy created for the book he wrote
called *Milk, Eggs, Vodka* (milkeggsvodka.com). The book
is a compilation of abandoned grocery lists that were discovered in grocery carts, on market floors, and in parking lots across the country.

"If we are what we eat, then this book reveals deep
truths about the average American (not to mention more
mundane truths like a surprising number of people
enjoy onions, and, for most people, banana and mayon-
naise are very, very difficult words to spell)," writes
Keaggy.

86. List-Making Tips

Aviva Goldfarb is a mother of two and the author and
founder   of   The   Six   O'Clock   Scramble
(thescramble.com), an online weekly menu planner and
cookbook. She is also the author of the cookbook *SOS!
The Six O'Clock Scramble to the Rescue: Earth Friendly, Kid-
Pleasing Meals for Busy Families.* She offers some great
advice when it comes to making a grocery list:

> When I was a girl, I remember my mom sitting down
> each week with her recipe boxes and making a shop-
> ping list. When I became a mom, I thought I could

never be that organized. So at first, I didn't try. I would walk the grocery aisles, letting items on the shelves inspire ideas for the week's dinners. The problem was, I would often get home and realize I was missing key ingredients, so I'd have to go shopping again or change my dinner plans. And the amount of food I was throwing away because I didn't get around to using it was appalling. I finally realized my mom had the right idea.

A weekly menu takes only about twenty minutes to prepare, but it saves us loads of time, stress, and money. Having a weekly menu allows us to shop only once each week for ingredients, avoiding those last-minute trips to the grocery store. And it saves us from having to think too much at the hectic dinner hour about what to prepare—the menu is ready. I usually plan my weekly menus on the weekends, but the day can vary depending on when I've used up all the food from last week's grocery trip.

Making your weekly menu and grocery list: Look at the calendar for the upcoming week to determine how many nights you will be eating dinner at home, and check whether there are any special events that you'll need to bring food or supplies to, such as snacks for games or parties, so you can get those items on your weekly grocery trip and save yourself a trip later.

I keep a file of recipes I want to try by subject, such as meat, fish, pasta, soups/stews, salads, sandwiches. If you prefer to use cookbooks, pull out the book(s) you plan to use for next week's meals. Select recipes for the upcoming week based on what's in season, your family's tastes, and your schedule. I usually choose one or two recipes with poultry or meat, one pasta, one soup, stew or salad, and one sandwich, wrap or an extra meatless meal. Check your refrigerator and pantry to see what items you'll need to buy for your menu, and add those items to a grocery list. Make sure to think about simple side dishes to serve with your meals, and plenty of fruit for snacks. Add whatever items your family will need for the upcoming week's breakfasts and lunches to your list, and you should be ready to go shopping!

I like to carry the grocery list and a pen in my hand or purse so I can check off items on my list as I buy them. Remember to have a healthy snack or a cup of coffee before you shop to give yourself the energy needed to buy your week's cooking supplies, and think of how much healthier your family will be eating and how much money you will save by preparing so many meals at home, rather than eating take-out, fast food, or going out to dinner.

87. Bag It Yourself

Save time at home by bagging your own groceries at the supermarket. You'll be mindful of bagging things that go in the same cabinet together. Once home, it will be easy to put things away or delegate bags to different members of your family.

88. See If Your Store Delivers

Many grocery stores deliver or have curbside pick up. If you purchase the same items each week, this can save you a lot of time. Check out Peapod.com or Netgrocer.com. Amazon.com also carries non-perishable food items. For household supplies, be sure to visit

Alice.com, which not only offers free shipping, but allows you to redeem online coupons as well.

89. Follow Strategies for Smarter Shopping

- Shop with a friend or partner. Split the list and meet in the middle.
- Grocery stores are often less crowded (sometimes almost empty!) early in the morning or late at night. Take advantage of the lull and do your shopping then. You won't have to wait in long checkout lines.
- Whenever possible, shop without your children. While we love them, kids can add lots of time (and money) to your shopping trip. Shop when your partner is home, or hire a babysitter once a week to watch them. You and a friend might also consider taking turns doing the shopping for both families.
- My grocery store has a deli kiosk where I can order my lunch meats to be sliced while I shop. This service is a big reason why I shop there. Standing in line at the deli counter can take up a lot of time. If your store doesn't offer this service, ask if you can call your order in ahead of time or if you can stop by the deli, place your order, and pick it up before you check out.

90. Skip the Clip

I love to save money at the grocery store, but sometimes I just don't have time to page through the stacks of coupons that come in Sunday's newspaper. Instead of spending a lot of time clipping coupons each week (and then being tempted by something you wouldn't normally buy because you have a coupon), skip the clip and let the coupons find you.

Couponmom.com is a comprehensive and free website that offers a coupon database, where you can search for the availability of coupons. For example, if Rice-a-Roni is on your meal plan, you can search Coupon Mom to see if a coupon for this product exists. If one does, Coupon Mom will give you the date and circular in which it appeared. Coupon Mom also matches existing coupons to grocery store sales. And the website offers a coupon alert service, where you can enter your favorite products and receive an email whenever a coupon for that item is available.

AFullCup.com is another free coupon site that matches coupons with sales at grocery stores. It also includes a database where you can search for coupons, and you can connect with other couponers in your area, sharing success stories and tips.

If you want to save money, but you don't want to spend the time matching coupons with sale prices and then figuring out if it's a good deal or not, consider the fee-based service TheGroceryGame.com. It does all the work for you, and it lets you know when a deal is a super deal so you can stock up.

Other websites include GrocerySavingTips.com, CouponCravings.com, and DealSeekingMom.com. Or you can get only the coupons you want at TheCoupon-Clippers.com or CouponClipperCrew.com.

If you do decide to take on the job of clipping

coupons, do it Mommy Multitask-style—while watching television. Or have your children help.

91. Choose the Best Store

Shop at stores that match competitors' advertised prices. Don't chase deals. It takes time and gas. It also saves time to stay loyal to one store. You will learn the store's layout and be able to quickly complete your shopping, and you will develop relationships with the manager, butcher, produce stockers, and bakery staff. They will often let you know about upcoming sales so you can stock up, and they will also let you know the best times of day to shop their stores.

If you do have to run to the store for one item, consider other places you can purchase that item. For example, most drug stores and gas stations carry milk and various grocery products. Parking is often easier, and you don't usually encounter long checkout lines.

92. If You Have to Bring the Kids, Have a Solid Plan

If you must bring your children to the grocery store, there are a few things to keep in mind. Don't go to the store near naptime or before a meal. Tired and hungry kids are more likely to have a tantrum. Make sure everyone visits the bathroom at home before you leave for the store, and ask your child again when you get to the store if he or she needs to go to the restroom before you start your shopping. Whenever possible, shop during one of the slower times for your store.

When my boys were little, I liked to park near the

cart return at my store so I didn't have to leave them unattended in the car or walk across a busy parking lot at the end of the shopping trip. You can also choose a store that offers help unloading groceries so you can concentrate on keeping the kids safe.

Make sure your child has eaten before you go, or bring a healthy snack with you so he or she can eat while you shop.

Set up rules before you go inside, including where you expect your child to be when you shop (walking next to you, sitting in the cart, etc.) and what to do if you get separated. Also establish how many items your child can choose and don't allow negotiating. To complete the shopping as quickly as possible, keep kids busy. Coupons can help with that.

My oldest son joined me on a recent trip to the grocery store, and I showed him how I had matched coupons to store sales. We purchased $125 worth of groceries for $42, and as he was helping me load the food into our car he said, "Mom, that was fun! Can I help you again?" I felt glad I had taken the time to tell him about coupons, and I've noticed he is paying more attention to our grocery store circulars.

While a teenager might grasp the money-saving benefit of coupons, they can be a good learning tool for any child.

Make it fun: When kids are young, turn coupons into a virtual scavenger hunt in which the child matches each coupon to the products on the shelf. The game will keep them occupied (so they aren't thinking about what they can ask you to buy). You can also play I Spy with shapes or colors in the store. This is a good game to play while waiting in a long checkout line.

Make it a math lesson: Older children can subtract the value of a coupon from the price of the product for a quick and easy subtraction drill. Then teach comparison-shopping by asking if the product with a coupon is a better deal than another brand. Older children can calculate savings in percentages and figure price per unit.

Make it real: When the shopping trip is over, talk to children about the total savings on the receipt. Then compare the savings to something that has value to them. For example, if you saved $17 using coupons, you can explain to your children that $17 is what it costs to have pizza on Friday nights.

Make a goal: Talk to children about what those savings mean to the family. Some families use the savings to create a vacation fund. Other families use the savings to afford little luxuries, such as a nice dinner out. For most of us, though, it just helps make ends meet.

Know your child's attention span and do everything you can to keep the length of your shopping visit within those parameters. If your child misbehaves and has a tantrum, do not feel bad about leaving your cart in the middle of the store and going home. If possible, let a member of the store staff know where the cart is and whether or not you can come back shortly to complete your shopping trip. Zero tolerance for misbehavior sends a message to your child and helps to prevent this from happening again. And be sure to reward good behavior with praise, a treat, or a ride on the mechanical horse. Positive reinforcement helps set the stage for the next shopping trip.

FIVE
Errands, Appointments, and On-the-Go

93. Run Errands Wisely

Think about your weekly errands—the grocery store, the drugstore, the mall, the gas station, the bank, the dry cleaner, the library. Now think about the errands you do on a less frequent basis, such as renewing licenses, making returns at stores, mailing packages at the post office, and enrolling your kids in classes. To save time on errands, ask yourself, are these errands all over town, or are they close to each other? If they are all over town, ask yourself, do they need to be all over town, or is there a more efficient way to accomplish everything? The branch or location you normally frequent may not always be the best choice.

When you do errands, never do just one. Combine and assign one day as errand day, when you get everything done at once. It can be helpful to shop at stores that offer one-stop services such as banking, pharmacy, or even dry cleaning.

94. Go Online

Is there any way your errand can be completed online or over the phone? Can you renew your library books to a date that fits your schedule better? Can you renew your driver's license or tags online or by mail?

Use your bank's online bill pay service, which is often free. You not only save the time it takes to write a check, you save a stamp. Better yet, automate your bills to be paid via direct checking draft or by credit card.

The U.S. Postal Service offers a convenient online

shipping service. You can purchase and print labels from your computer and even have the mail carrier pick up your packages right at your door. Think of how much time this will save during the busy holiday season when everyone is waiting in line!

95.   Book It Now, Book It Early, and Book It Together

When you're a busy mom, it seems like you're always making appointments for your family, including the four-legged members—the hairdresser, the doctor, the dentist, the orthodontist, the vet, the dog groomer.

Now think about how you could accomplish these appointments more efficiently. Always request the first appointment of the day with your doctor, dentist, ortho-dontist, veterinarian, or hairstylist. This will reduce your waiting time. And don't be afraid to call ahead and see if the doctor or stylist is running behind.

If possible, schedule appointments—such as teeth cleaning, haircuts, or physicals—for your entire family on the same day. I even make appointments for my boys' annual dental checkup at the same time, with two differ-ent hygienists in chairs right next to each other. We're in and out in a flash!

Also, make your next appointment before you leave your last appointment. Those coveted time slots (after school or first thing in the morning) are often hard to get. If you book them weeks or even months in advance, you have a better chance of scoring one. If you discover you have a conflict, call right away to reschedule. And make sure you will be receiving a reminder call or email.

It can be hard to make an appointment that is six months away, but it's one less phone call you need to make later.

Finally, choose to patronize service providers who are respectful of your time. If your stylist keeps you waiting for forty-five minutes before your hair appointment—especially if it happens more than once—let him or her know your time is valuable.

The same goes for doctors. Remember, you are hiring them. If your doctor is chronically late, consider finding another healthcare provider.

96. Call Ahead

Frequent restaurants that offer reservations (often called call-ahead seating today). Or call before you leave home to see how long the wait is. Sometimes, even if a restaurant doesn't accept reservations, they will add your name to the list if they know you are on your way.

97. Traffic Tips

- Traffic is generally lighter on weekdays between 10:00 a.m. and noon or 1:00 to 3:00 p.m.
- When possible, avoid shopping districts during the holiday season.
- Before you head out, check the website BeatTheTraffic.com for alerts on slow traffic, incidents, events, and construction. The information is free, although you can sign up for their paid service, which will send alerts to your cell phone.

98.   Create a Worth Remembering Journal

Have you ever gone to the library, video rental place, or book store and forgotten which movie or book you wanted to bring home? I used to be guilty of this, and I have wasted so much time browsing the shelves, certain I'll stumble across whatever it is I wanted to get.

To avoid doing this again, I created a *Worth Remembering Journal* that I keep in my purse. It saves me time, because I can quickly check inside for the titles of books and movies I have written down to remind myself to get. I even jot down the names of wines I've had at friends' homes or restaurants that I like.

My *Worth Remembering Journal* is also the place where I record favorite dishes at restaurants as well as dishes to not order again. When my son was in his macaroni and cheese phase, one local restaurant made it in a way that he didn't like. Another sprinkled minced parsley on top, which meant he wouldn't eat it. It was hard to remember which place did what, so I started writing it down so I could be sure to order it just the way he liked it (so we didn't have to send it back or I didn't spend my time picking parsley out of melted cheese).

99.   Run Errands with Kids at Your Own Risk

Running errands with children in tow can add a high degree of difficulty (not to mention more time) to the equation. Sometimes, however, it's unavoidable.

If you are bringing the kids on errand day, try to keep your number of stops to a minimum. Getting in and out of the car with strollers, car seats, diaper bags, etc., is tiring for both mom and child.

Give your child the plan for the day. If he or she knows you are making three stops, it will help avoid the are-we-done-yet questions. Once you've told your child what to expect from you, then tell him or her what you expect. "Don't touch," for example, and tell them what the consequences will be if they disobey. Be prepared to follow through with the consequences. Nothing is more ineffective than false threats.

Avoid running errands around your child's naptime to reduce the rist of embarrassing and time-consuming meltdowns. Be sure to feed your child before you go, but also bring a snack and a drink. Kids will always get hungry, especially if you are in a store with food or you drive by a fast-food restaurant. (It's a good idea to keep a few nonperishable foods in your car for emergencies anyway.)

When my boys were little, I chose stores that were child friendly (i.e., the ones where they got free cookies, balloons, or stickers). This always made the outing at least a little easier.

100. Use Pictures to Turn Errands into Teaching Moments

Lindsay Ballard, mom of two, came up with a fun way to ease the pain of errands with a toddler:

> Running errands with a toddler is about as easy as herding cats. Those of you who have or have had young children know exactly what I'm talking about. Those of you who haven't reached this phase of your

life have absolutely no idea. It's probably better to keep it that way if you think kids are in your future.

All mamas know to bring a few small toys, a sippy cup, and a snack when they are running errands. If you didn't realize the vital necessity of these items, you will certainly never forget how much "fun" you had the first time you forgot them. Toddler meltdown, much?

I try to get as many errands run in one trip as I can so I don't have to run around town with Zack every day. Trust me when I say that it's better for everyone involved. However, it got to be difficult because after a few stops he'd start complaining that he wanted to go home and would start sassing me, and it was driving me crazy!

I finally realized that Zack didn't understand that we only had a few more stops left to make. It was a concept that he wasn't able to grasp or visualize. One morning, I came up with his very own list of errands we needed to run, complete with pictures representing each store or activity, so that he could "see" what we were doing.

With this list, Zack is able to see the tasks that we need to complete. When we finish an errand, he draws a line through it and tells me what's next on the list.

Zack's errand list has made our shopping trips so much easier. Not only is he able to gauge how much longer we have to shop, but also I think it makes him feel like he's participating by helping Mama know where to go next.

Try it next time you need to run some errands. It's guaranteed to make your trip a little bit easier, and I know we all need as much help as we can get!

What's in Your Car Bag?

OK, so you're not jet-setting across the country. You're just going to the grocery store. You may be tempted to hop in the car and go, but let's just see what's in your car bag (or handbag) for those just-in-case scenarios. Grab your bag and let's see how you do!

1. If you have a pen, you get one point. (Keep it out and use it for scorekeeping.)
2. Cell Phone—2 points
3. Tissue—2 points
4. Calendar/Planner—3 points (+1 point if it has dates/information entered)
5. Pad of paper—3 points (+1 if it is a Post-It note pad)
6. Lip balm—4 points
7. Safety Pin—4 points
8. Anti-bacterial Gel or Wipes—5 points
9. Tide to Go Pen or other spot remover—10 points
10. Children's Tylenol/Pain Reliever—10 points

101. Start an Errand Co-op

Instead of stressing out over errands, consider starting an errand co-op with a friend or other neighborhood moms. One mom can watch the children while another runs the errands.

102. Put It in the Car

As you collect items that need to be dropped off, returned, or picked up, put them in your car so you won't

How'd You Do?

If you earned 36 to 46 points, you are "Amazing Mom," killing thousands of germs with a swipe of your anti-bacterial wipe! Unfortunately, you are also the mom other moms love to hate, but so what? Let them—you rock! Still, try to be kind when they ask if you have a tissue!

If you earned 22 to 35 points, you are "Amazing Mom's Understudy." Some days you're really on your game, but other days it's apparent that you're not the star. Don't fret. One day it will be *your* pad of paper that everyone wants to borrow.

If you earned 10 to 21 points, you are "MacGyver Mom," a super-resourceful mom who can work wonders with a safety pin and a wet wipe (that you pocketed from the Crab Shack). You travel light and make do, and you're teaching your children to be self-reliant.

If you earned less than 10 points, you are "Fun Mom!" So what if you only carry a cell phone and lip balm? (Bobbi Brown Lip Balm to be precise!) That's OK. Since you are so much fun to be around, the other moms will take care of you. Besides, you have the best stories!

forget anything at home. Put a basket or collapsible bin in your trunk and put anything that needs to be returned (along with the receipt) in it. Or get a tote bag to hold dry cleaning and put it in your car. As you finish reading library books or watching rented videos, put them in a bag in your car so you don't have to search all over your house on the day you're going. Another handy idea is to keep restaurant, dry cleaning, or haircut coupons in your glove box, so you have them handy when you need them.

103. Create Busy Bags for Every Occasion

In addition to a car bag, smart moms pack busy bags filled with goodies to occupy little kids. You can create an all-purpose busy bag or bags for specific occasions, such as eating out, going to church, errand day, or trips to visit relatives (especially those who don't have small children living there: no toys!). Items used only for these special occasions will hold your child's attention better than just tossing some of their well-used toys in the car.

When dining out, pack a bag that includes crayons, paper, coloring books, restaurant games (Family Time Fun makes great games that involve the items on your table), a deck of cards, pipe cleaners, or bingo. Think outside the box, too, and pack an old calculator. (Ask your child to add up the total cost of every appetizer on the menu.) Or bring a stopwatch and time how long it takes for your food to come.

Keep young children occupied in church with a bag that includes quiet activities, such as crayons and coloring books, lift-the-flap books, paper dolls, or lacing cards.

On errand day, have a bag of activities your child can do in the car or while sitting in a shopping cart or stroller.

104. Keep Necessities in the Car

Mom Candi Wingate offers some advice for organizing the car:

Sometimes, the most challenging part of my day is

just getting out the door with all the necessary lunches, briefcases, backpacks, sports gear, and permission slips for the day ahead. I've started keeping a plastic bin in the trunk of my car that contains all the sports gear for the coming week. This way, I never forget the tennis racquet, baseball glove, or team jersey for the upcoming practices or games.

I keep necessities in my car and replace the items at regular intervals. I always have snacks, bottled water, and hand sanitizer, bug spray, sunscreen, and other necessities at my fingertips. I find that it saves me a ton of time to pack all of these items at once, rather than having to scramble for granola bars or sunscreen as we're rushing out the door.

105. Make the Most of Wait Time

Kate Hare makes sure she has something to do whenever she has to wait anywhere:

> I use a portable file and fill it with some of the paperwork I need to do. I sort mail and school papers while I'm waiting during a ballet lesson or swim practice, such as banking and card statements to check later against my Quicken downloads, and doctor statements that I need to file with our insurance, etc., and then I sort them into the proper file. I also have a file for "calls to make" (because the bill doesn't look right or because they need our insurance information or I thought I'd cancelled some account) and a "bills to pay" folder.

JOIN
The Conversation!

Congratulations! You are now a card-carrying member of the Five-Minute Mom's Club.

Visit www.fiveminutemomsclub.com and join our community and our conversation. It's like the virtual carpool line.

We're here to help you accomplish your goals, cheer you on, and support your commitment to leave Super Mom behind. We believe moms are the best source of information, and we hope you will share your best five-minute tip with our group. See you soon!

About the author

Stephanie Vozza is an expert in time-saving organization and is nationally recognized as the "Time-Saving Mom." She loves coming up with quick solutions for the tasks that cause moms stress.

Stephanie has contributed her organization and time-saving tips to *Parents, Woman's Day, Family Circle, Nick Jr.,* and *Pregnancy* magazines as well as in articles for the Associated Press. She pens a monthly column, "The Five-Minute Mom," which is carried in parenting publications across the country and also serves as a guest blogger on several websites, including the Huffington Post. Stephanie has been a featured speaker at the Michigan International Women's Show and regularly speaks to PTA and Mother's Groups.

As founder and president of The Organized Parent, a company with a mission to make moms' lives easier, Stephanie offers products to busy moms looking to organize their life. In 2009, she joined FranklinCovey, global leader in time management, as the company's Busy Mom Guru and regularly blogs for the company's Get Organized Community. In 2010, Stephanie was named Kids/Organization Expert for Sears' Manage My Life website. Stephanie was also named Organizing Guru for giggle.com, a store for new parents. In addition, The